China, the Pearl, and I

by Dalita I. Alex

CHINA
INTERCONTINENTAL
PRESS

图书在版编目（CIP）数据

珍珠 = China, the Pearl, and I/ (瑞士) 亚历克斯 (Alex, D.I.) 著. —北京: 五洲传播出版社, 2004.10

ISBN 7-5085-0604-9

I. 珍… II. 亚… III. 随笔－作品集－瑞士－现代－英文 IV. I522.65

中国版本图书馆 CIP 数据核字 (2004) 第 105170 号

珍珠

著　　者：(瑞士) 达丽塔·I·亚历克斯
责任编辑：邓锦辉
编　　辑：吴娅民　张行军
装帧设计：田　林
版式制作：北京原色印象文化艺术中心
出版发行：五洲传播出版社 (北京海淀区莲花池东路北小马厂 6 号　邮编：100038)
承 印 者：北京华联印刷有限公司
开　　本：787 × 1092mm　1/16
印　　张：10.25
字　　数：100 千
版　　次：2004 年 10 月第 1 版
印　　次：2004 年 10 月第 1 次印刷
书　　号：ISBN 7-5085-0604-9/I·46
定　　价：59.00 元

CONTENTS

SECTION ONE

Contents

SECTION ONE

Our Endeavours Were Treasured with Enriched Experiences

I was in a daydream that Thursday afternoon, sitting in front of my computer, asked to write down the story of my many frequent trips to Mainland China, my lived experiences, events and escapades with the Chinese people. Those were cherished memories, enthralled, full of adventure; souvenirs rich of unrivalled experiences, of conspicuous flagrant knowledge through discovery of the old and the new. [i]

I was to encounter "the old" with such an avid curiosity. As for "the new" I had to find and appreciate its novelty slowly but duly, mostly coming to understand the "Tao" – the path of my life – a word that I learned in the Chinese philosophy, henceforth a good term to express my indentations during my business trips in China and my itinerary in general, which I ardently believe were enhanced by the cosmic influence in harmonising and leading the pre-eminent changes of my life. Notwithstanding every visit had its capital influence to shape up my life, through its experiences and endeavours. Every visit had to play a decisive role on my financial situation and social establishment, to balance our decisions, to set forth and appreciate the influence of my encounters, thus accepting the givings and relinquishing their results as the fruits of our endeavours. [ii]

The sun was already high up in the sky, a good indication that many hours had elapsed, ever since I took my writing. I laid down my pencil, feeling little bit swarming in my senses. I stood up, having a very strong envy to sip a cup of tea, an envy of a hot

---

i Dalita I. Alex, *Ageless*, where this concept was explained in deep detail.

ii cfr. Alex, page 225-237. I apply this though here in another context.

liquid, to adulterate my throat thus to mitigate and pacify my dried lips. But beneath that sudden desire there was also an act, an urge to enhance and impel a perceptive incitement of my forgotten memories. Thirsty and impulsive, I hastily entered the kitchen to prepare my magic drink to stir and excite my impulses by evoking my memories. It can be realized through the sound of music, the touch of an article, the sight of a place, the smell of the earth after a rainfall, or the aroma of a food. I think Orientals are more prone to the awakening of their conscious mind in general than Occidentals, and me being prone to the philosophy of the Orient I had the eagerness and the preparation to evoke my unfathomable subjective feelings, to induce them to realisation and enlightenment, whenever there was an occasion to celebrate.

I run across a panoply of all kinds of tea, a variety of English tea and especially Chinese tea. A collection of cha that I had the useful habit to drink some of these beneficial drinks in my daily diet. I watched for a while my collection at the back of the shelf, as if I was noticing them for the first time. Indeed I was overhauling them under another light and another dimension. Exploring them from the shelf, where I had exhibited a rich collection of my recollections, scrutinizing and observing the reminiscence and the wishfulness of those little objects: tea cups and potteries of all sizes, very big with lids, middle ones and very small ones, made of porcelain or clay (ref. details about tea drinking to go back *Ageless*). I started to summon up the where, why and how! Most of them were tokens of friendship, given to me at special events or bought at different occasions, which were opportunities of delectable experiences during our trips and tours to Shanghai, Beijing, Fujian, Hainan, Guangdong, Hong Kong, Jiangsu and numerous cities and famous villages.

Many names were coming to my mind, as well as friendly faces and welcoming serene sites, hamlets, dwellings and localities. They were starting to play their magic by soliciting and boosting impressions and feelings which were standing out of my lived moments and indentations of the places I visited, that had an impact on me: the little shops, the corner of a department store, the souvenir shops, or the arcade of a big hotel where I bought something impulsively.

My frequent trips to those different towns and cities were rare opportunities to come across their various kind of tea, peculiar and rare, in one word the art, the pleasure of the tea ceremony (ref. to book *Ageless*). Finally, getting across and around my china-sets, I chose a white porcelain teacup with the motif of a lotus, in pink and red hues. I touched that empty teacup for a few seconds, to see if the vibrations were having any effect on me. My invisible vibrations of energy were at work! My awareness was capturing those sensations through my nervous system, at the very deep of my being. I looked at the cup again, so immaculate and white, reminding me of a very famous Chinese painting, a drawing which represented a young aristocrat, wearing a white silken gown, with rose and pink lotus on her chest. For the first time I wanted the cup to luxuriate in a talk, to gratify and indulge its story and itinerary, before dropping into my house. The suggestive drawing and motif on the cup did remind me of the place where the tea was bought. "That's good," I was telling myself. "That's wonderful!" Details, even the slightest details, were stirring and arousing in my head. Scenes and past-images were quickly inducing the impulses to my memory.

Now my hot water was hot enough to make an exquisite tea. I chose a very special tea bought to us from Beijing. I was told that the Emperors of China used to drink from that tea, very small leaves almost reddish brown, spicy, a bitter foretaste. I used it only for very special occasions, knowing that I cannot find similar teas in Zurich, since it was a very special blend, just like our itineraries of special mood and sensation. I smiled watching the hot and humid fume escape from the cha pot. How many times did I share such consecrated drinks, aromas of my happy moments with Chinese friends, corporate and passers-by? I can not recall! Yet one thing I can think and align, insisting about its value, as being the simplest and healthiest drink of friendship, beatitude and grace made of pure water and herbs.

My Choice of the Title

A human being has got its subjective and objective insight, and one accomplishes the other. The more balance there is in these two elements, the better is the harmony of the person, and its resistance to the encountered situations. When one is too objective, too much down-to-earth, being Cartesian, somewhere on the line, he will have to encounter and come into conflict with some of the questions ensued that happen on, and the answers could not always be explained on the objective level, knowing for sure that science hasn't the answers of all questions even though much is being achieved through it. The same purpose is for the very subjective persons, who detach themselves from the earthly dispassionate open-minded unbiased realities, especially when committed to issues running across, and conveying the assessment of his innermost feelings to choices, aspirations, longings and desires. So my choice of a title was neither very far from my mind nor from my heart, regarding and taking also into account the subject I was to reckon. This issue had developed and was waiting for the moment to dawn, to shine and spread like the rainbow after a rain, which glimmers and decorates the sky with its colourful inspiration. Henceforth my enthusiasm and awakening of the moments was flashing across my mind, to unfold and bring forth the title "China, the Pearl, and I."

This conspicuous and propitious title is the true concept of my story, making an all-out effort in my attempt not to give the impression that I am being conceited or fanciful in the choice of this heading.

Before visiting Mainland China, yet much before that, I was incited through books, magazines, and impelled by documentary films about the Far East and its alluring culture. Television was not what it is today, full of diversified information of cultural, social and political issues, not to undermine the magic of the internet, a world by itself, "a world fair" piled and stored of incessant information for the lucky new generation and the lesser young public, for intellectuals as well as for businessmen. It is also a rescue wheel for the ones who want to be entertained, henceforth rendering a tremendous service for the new and the old generation to benefit. For my generation cinema was the means for enlightenment and education, thus taking us to faraway lands and ideas, concepts and fashion, for us to think, to compare, and to dream. I was, beyond a shadow, assuredly influenced by films and mediated shots. In a very reserved society with a narrow-minded approach on different issues having to do with social matters on hot topics of love and money and general conduct where our generation was suffering mainly of the guilt of desire and the attempt to make decisions.

I was a teenager when I first saw the film *The king and I*, its major actors being Yul Brynner and Deborah Kerr. It is an American film made in Hollywood that I saw for the first time in the 1960s.

Notwithstanding I understood and analysed that film with the insight of a young girl, who was seeing for the first time the Asian continent and its exotic customs, I will not forget and undermine the respect and admiration embodied in a platonic love, and the attraction of a European woman to an Asian king. They had a deep affection for one another, despite the great differences in their culture. The romance and the platonic love in that relation was mostly and mainly alluring to my young and innocent heart, although being so much in contrast with today's superficial and unsubstantiated love stories that have one aim: momentary attraction and sex. Images have so much impact on children, the same thing happened to me.

Henceforth were the obvious rebound of my desire and its reverberation to enhance and boost the itinerary I had to take to meet the "Silk Road", an innocent allot which was first drawn in my heart as an spiritual aura, then in my head. My path had to make a turn of 360 degrees on the compass of my life. It was undoubtedly an innocent desire which did not need to exert any will or guilt conscious to bring forward memories of my longings to life.

The protagonist of the film *The King and I* possessed qualities that made her more conspicuous. Anna, the heroin of the film, was an English teacher appointed by the king and the courtier, to furnish a Western education to his court elements (children and courtship). She was a British citizen, educated, knowledgeable and elegant, possessing a critical and outspoken character (something that was not conceivable in that epoch, especially for a woman), in one word a courageous person. Her origin had its capital importance of course, to give her more pride and make her feel sure of herself. She was well aware that she belonged – although very far away from home – to a solid nation in the 19th century Britain, which was in full expansion, an empire, where the sun did not set down on its territory. Britain claimed to have by far the largest merchant ships all around the world, war fleets, marine ships, overpowering all other nations in Europe, and the Asian world, an ambitious programme and requisite for an empire which was at odds with the Asian empire. Already in the 19th century, Britain had its industrial revolution, was ambitious to overpower other nations and to endorse a modernised economical welfare and education. He had revolutionised and washed away the old system, and brought forth novelty to a world which was emerging towards acceptance, with some reticence. British already had freedom of thought and ideology. Their famous *Gazette* newspaper is a very good example, possessing the privilege of criticising and accepting the new and the different. Britain could also boast of having a more defined social ethics and courtesy and a more pronounced occidental decorum and protocol, not undermining its modernised and organised economy of defined statues. All of which were somehow in contrast to the Asian world, in China with the Manchu emperors modernisation was almost forgotten, where freedom was conducted through a king or an emperor and dealt with the different aspects and issue of social etiquette, political problems, refined social welfare through religious leaders and philosophers, whilst centuries long they were known, especially for the Chinese, as innovators, inventors and creators in many fields, which had to open new possibilities and innovative ideas to reshape and enhance to the quick development of the other countries, mainly Middle Eastern cities and the Occident.

The colonialist British of that epoch, indeed, besides being conceited and ambitious, were also conservative, in their dogmatic demeanours, while Asians in general were more traditionalists, therefore conserving an immobile empire. Asian sovereigns, especially Chinese emperors, besides being the most powerful leaders and the most dominant and authoritative Asian emperors, they were also the law, the one who was bearing the consciousness of the people; and if that emperor had a consciousness and a candour based on many-century-old religious-and social-bound consciousness, immobile and without any hint of the new fangleness and innovativeness in current duties, and in the aspiration of his people, then the outcome would be somehow stagnating and conflicting to the outside world. A new world was running towards openness, exchange of ideas, business and trade, sharing of knowledge, thus trying to minimise differentiation and contretemps through new and different concepts in ideologies and welfare.

China, or Fulfillment of Desire

Today, when I wanted to write my book about my lived and cherished experiences on China, yet like a film running in my head and heart, I decided to single out and opt for this title *China, the Pearl, and I*.

China is and plays the host: people who were committed and thriven to wave and brandish their country's successful ascension and tremendous change. The immobile empire was only a past history. While the present is a dawn projected towards bigger changes for a promising future.

I was to carry out and to treat my impressions. The entity was holistic, powerful and in full expansion.

The personification of the Pearl element in my adventures is of capital importance, and what ever beaten about it was the tool, the mean, a river of strings, a cascade of attraction, in one word the reason to be.

The Roman general Julius Caesar once has said, reporting about his victory in a battle, "Veni, vidi, vici." (I came, I saw, I conquered.) While me the "I", the one who came, saw and tried to conquer through her appreciation and esteem through consideration and regard to the brilliant and industrious peoples of Asia.

I have to display my feelings and impressions like an artist, free from any influence protected in her "self", drawing her objective and subjective encounters and feelings, attributed to a world centred on its own axis, so vast and so big. Impressions are my true feelings, free from any outside solicited assessment. There existed only China and me, detached from the other worlds, which were so far away. I did not need to judge or to compare with the other worlds that I had to encounter during my life, since its vast dimension and diversified world is an computation, an appraisal rated to itself, the one and only.

"I"

As for the "I", the guest had the privilege, the heed, henceforth the luck, to hanker after that host country called "China."

Being modest and humble does not and must not inhibit your feelings towards esteem, appreciation, or praise. On the other hand it is much more difficult to keep a low profile when you know you are privileged, and acting with modesty, actually knowing that you do not have to comply to a ratio or to a superlative status.

This is how the title of my book was forged and with it the undermining folds of that beautiful story of an European woman in the old Asia, who had so much compassion and eagerness to understand, to love, and to aspire after that country's culture, its king, and people. The exotic and the different did not fear her; and through the eyes of love she saw that she was the same and the equal.

The parallel of my story is so much like that young European woman. During my frequent visits I was hankering with the old and new China, henceforth I had the privilege to have been acquainted to his culture, his philosophy, his creativity, and his people. I had experienced moments of happiness that neither money nor wealth could compensate, and got immeasurable experiences full of velvety emotions.

The title *China, the Pearl, and I* engulfs all the magic of a freely expressed book, an alluring story of an admirer, a romantic, open-minded, impartial person. "China" being the Emperor, the Majesty, "the Pearl" being the queen and "I", the humble protagonist.

Growing up through Vivid Images

Years went by, that teenage girl grew up little by little. She developed her natural potentials, her insight and aspirations expanded, hence shaped her innermost feelings to ride to the door of the new and the unknown. Innermost feelings made her realise that her time had come to share her life to love and assign to the man of her heart. A man who was of European origin, who had looked for her around the world (from Brazil to the Middle East, Europe till Japan). He was guided through his angels who led him to the only path and the right moment, thus ensuring him to meet her, which would be initially crowned with the concept of "happy happening." Finally having found her, he married her in an interval of two weeks, incredible but true.

Our marriage was celebrated like every young girl would have dreamt of. Comely and wonderful in the Armenian Apostolic church as if angels were singing for our timeless happiness. We were blessed, because we were the couple who had the approval of the cosmos and of course, not to forget having had the consent and acquiescence of our parents. As for the duration, the timing of our encounters was four days less than a month. Initially that became a subject of polemic among friends and relatives. No one was willing to believe in our story. During a Christian marriage ceremony, the priest or the archbishop puts crowns made of gold and precious stones on our heads, symbolising the idea of the church to crown us like the king and queen of our initial family. Thus embody the sole power of a family. But in our case, I had the ultimate conviction and the quintessence that our union was of another dimension. To epitomise my conviction metaphorically, thus display and lay off my feelings on that special moment, having had the sensation that we were carrying actually a tangible discernible golden crown and a cosmic necklace around our necks, whose beads formed a river of pearls that were to become the path on which we had to walk hand in hand, my newly wedded husband and I.

We got married at the church, in front of our beloved parents, siblings, cousins, and nephews and five hundred guests and people of all standing and of different origin. We took our vows to love and cherish each other in health and in sickness, in richness or in poverty, to be loyal, respectful, caring and loving towards each other, amen. All these were beautiful, and stood up to be true considering our happy marriage of three long decades with our three healthy and beautiful children, dragging them in our incessant adventurous life full of unprecedented alluring, mysterious and exotic events, affirmative years whose repercussions I had to yield and concede to.

So my opportunity to go to those Far Eastern countries was being presented. I wanted dearly to see the Far East with its unfathomable, abstruse, and concealed sights, landscapes, soil, water, people. Everything there was attracting me like the magnetic field of the north and south pole. Of course my husband having already experienced those sights so many years before me; he had the sacred privileges to guide me, through the coming events and happenings, to make my childhood desire a dream come true.

The choice of my heart, my beloved husband was an European man, who was to take me to Eastern lands, to explore and experience along with me, the woman of his life on the reefs of this Far Eastern river, especially to China. He wanted to start establishing a happy and sound family, in stretched new horizons, beneath new shining stars, inundated and blessed by new hopes; to endeavour in the unknown, the different and the new. I never regretted my choice thank God, since through this marriage I was discovering the man and the land, which were to nourish my enthusiastic and passion-ate soul and a curious mind and above all bring forth my offspring, my unrivalled and unique pearls in the lands of pearl.

I will unfold and stretch my enriching experiences, observations and definitions in this diversified field on the alluring and complex human nature. I will display and expand my observations with the old and new architecture, disseminate their culture regarding art, literature, music, and outfit. Henceforth the direct influence and awareness enabled me to incorporate their philosophy, promulgate the technique of their martial art with its impingement upon, and partake of their traditional medicine based on very rare and exotic elaborate herbs – more than 2,000 plant-based herbal medicine – recalling mostly and dearly the occasions being a party to their exquisite and lavish culinary art. Those were opportunities of unequalled treasure; I was living the contemporary story of a big nation which has a continuous history of statehood, religion, and culture stretching back into a history of 6,000 years. Henceforth to find out the old and the different China that till then I had learned and discovered only through history books, which were not so tangible and palpable.

When destiny knocked on my door with its cosmic staff, it was an invitation, to initiate me to the magic of discovery and adventure. I was given the unrivalled opportunity to learn, explore, and put into evidence the theories about the Far East, especially China, on its sites and spots, on its main streets, temples and pagodas, palaces, its harbours and houses of hundreds of years old, meanwhile discern and solemnise new faces of people that could not alter their spirit no matter the regime or the political influence. They were committed and assessed to be brave, creative, and inventive. I will try to elaborate my cherished moments as unequalled treasure all along my book, which I will entitle *China, the Pearl, and I*.

I think if we are to feel at home in the world, we shall have to admit Asia to equality in our thoughts, not only politically but culturally. What changes this will bring about I do not know, but I am convinced that they will be profound and of the greatest importance.

Bertrand Russell, *History of the Western Philosophy*

The Pearl: My Path, My Tao, an Allegiance to the Pearl

The Pearl Road

There was a "Silk Road" in ancient China and there was also a "Pearl Road" which dates back 2,000 years ago, but reopened its road at the second half of the 20th century. It elongates from the north-east coast, till the south-west coast of the mainland crossing mainly the cities of Guangzhou, Nanjing, Nanchang, Shanghai, Hangzhou, Beijing, and the Hainan Island. China's big potential was always its natural resources: countless lakes and rivers, crossing these provinces. A fertile land young, lush, dense, and rich, a prolific soil needed endlessly to be explored and made into richness. The 19th century writer Alphonse Daudet in his famous book *Lettres de mon moulin* spoke about the earth and the richness that lies within and talked to his offsprings, urging them the love, the painstaking and the commitment to find one's compensation into the blessed soil.

Invoking My Memories

Being a mother, a supportive and promoting wife, I had the sacred duty to be a helping-hand during and after our trips and long stays, to stand by, organise, and deal with the trade and the enterprise of my husband, who was at the head of this interesting and enriching business, "the pearl business" with discreet intention and self-effacement.

This reality was the main reason which brought us in contact with China as the source of "the pearl." It was not a discovery as with Japan but rather a revived trade line, which was an ensuing assignment of concern, an allegiance, a responsibility to be dealt with care, to undertake its different steps of cultivating, manufacturing and industrialising the product, much before marketing and selling procedure issued and ensued at work.

Let me trace back to the events and the happenings which reshaped our path that took us to the land of all possibilities, of origin and creativity. Henceforth our Chinese adventure started back then, in the early 1970s, when we were still staying in Japan.

Hailing the Far East

Initially the first itinerary of my Far Eastern adventure started with Japan, where I stayed for six years. Japan's contribution was by and large as important as China. Of course it had another taste and another flavour. There is so much paradox in those two nations, being very close but not the same. Indeed they have some points in common, but relating to individual characters and behaviours so different and far apart. This is why I assume Chinese never associate any resemblance with the Japanese.

I spoke their language, and felt very much at home, being a "Geijinson" foreigner. What I appreciated most was their dignity through an unsurpassed politeness, their creative intelligence and innovative mind; not to undermine their modesty and their attitude to venerate the knowledgeable, the new, the better, and the best.

What's essential for them was to advance, to build a better future. And the results were rewarding and could be apprehended for their status later on.

I was blessed by becoming twice a mother in the land of Nippon. Henceforth my days were more concentrated on my family issues and obligations, which were the incessant duty, a rewarding toil of a mother and a wife, in comparison rather to the dormant business woman, the hibernated person that I was then. I could not be as demonstrative and undertaking as my business trips and stays in China. I could hardly enhance in my personal endeavours, which needed a few more years to be undertaken. Henceforth China was to replenish and ample those desires.

Changing Itineraries

My life in Japan was also very enriching and interesting. Almost every week we encountered something new. Notwithstanding being my first Far Eastern excursion everything was totally new for me. Their culture, especially their samurai stories, was fascinating for me. The altogether different language, bearing in mind, I had not yet run across, seemingly, the other very interesting yet difficult language, which was the Chinese language and its writing characters, which were the basis of the Japanese Kanji block writing! Their food had another taste, another smell. Basic ingredients are rice and the famous Soya beans, an important nutritional food rich in mineral and calcium which was prepared and cooked in all forms and taste. Japanese had very simple taste and they never complicated things. Their architecture, especially the old ones, pagoda or palace in Nara and Kyoto (old capitals of Japan) are mainly influenced by Chinese architecture and Zen Buddhism. Taking the example of a modest house of fifty to seventy square meters, the rooms are divided with paper sliding doors and floors covered with tatami (a kind of carpet made of straw). Initially I am very keen to knowledge and curious towards the new, especially things related or committed to tradition, to culture, and symbolic issues such as the kimono, and their hierarchy ensuing and adhering distinctively to rank, social statues and position, sometimes ensuing mysterious and passionate stories related to their wearers. This was the Kimono, the national gown of Japan. They could be in silk and of course in cotton for light summer days. These outfits are a pride to own and a privilege to the wearer. Kimono in its form is very strict but so beautiful in its lines, just like their houses and gardens in which everything is clean cut. I was thrilled and more than happy to meet all these cultural displays which was such an enriching experience.

Very seldom we had the visit of relatives and friends from abroad, or even having had the chance to be acquainted with new faces. So you can imagine my happiness when I met and shook hands with the big and renowned French singer Charles Aznavour and his group when he gave a concert in Osaka. In another occasion we shook hands with the group of the British Royal Ballet. Or during another event I met the very famous and renowned late Russian violinist David Oystrach, whose Godly concert was an unprecedented joy and an enticement to classical music.

Living in a very cosmopolitan area, we would meet foreigners of many different nationalities. The Kobe Club was the key to that kind of encounters, since being foreigners ourselves, we had this ardent need to meet people which were in the same situation as us.

One thing that amazes me even today, after so many years that even Chinese residents were considered foreigners, peculiar human relation where history can only have a satisfactory explanation. I also have another observation to be accounted – when I was still living in Kobe, the Japanese were not as open-minded and Westernised as today. Their attitude changed after the 1970s by educating themselves to the reality of other countries, which broadened their horizon.

Going to a new place for sightseeing or for business was also in my weekly surprises. When I first visited Japan the sights that impressed me most was my visit to the sight of the Fuji Mountain (the Fuji Yama or the Fuji San 4,500 meters high) for the first time, coming out of the clouds so condescending and majestic. As for my second souvenir was my first visit to the sites of the pearl-farms, an unequalled pleasure of curiosity and amazement. Those were to become the site, the locations, the path of discern that my husband and I had to pick out, week after week, at the discovery of the bountiful unfathomable pearls, the natural sea and lake treasures of our unbounded earth.

The Encounter

A Chinese delegation from Shanghai had the cordial visit to our office. It was a promising spring day, sunny and warm, an auspicious day to start a new venture. Kobe that time was the fifth largest city of Japan, situated on the east coast of the country, roughly in the centre of Honshu Island (Japan's main island). It was a city whose characteristic and importance was mainly for its busy port which attracted many foreigners. And of course among many other attractive businesses, it had become the centre of pearl business mainly because of the presence of different kinds of pearls on the market. Cultured pearls were from different cities: of native product, and also pearls from abroad, like the south sea pearls, or the Australian pearls that Japan that time had a direct purchase and control on the output of these products. Another major factor for being the pearl centre was the presence of the pearl inspection

officers, controlled by the government. These inspectors, who besides being government employees, were experts having the full possibility and the potential to decide on
the quality of the pearls and grade them accordingly. In case they did not comply with
the drawn criteria, they were all rejected as disqualified pearls banned to be exported
overseas. This is how inferior quality pearls could not leave the country. Due to this
inspection bureau the Japanese pearl had won the esteem and respect of the world
market, enabling them to keep rather a stable price and quality control, which had to
adjust itself with the recurring inflation policy of the market.

The city's charm included to the fact that it could easily be commuted, either for
land, sea, or air, that gave of course better advantages regarding tourists, merchants
and residents. Kobe was also famous for its many festivals, but the main one was the
Kobe Festival. It is held around the third Sunday of May. The main event of the
festival comprised a parade. One year my family and I had participated in that parade,
henceforth the Kobe festival was commemorated and remembered with another
dimension ensuing an enticement and a momentous decoy.

Pearl, the Queen of Gems

My husband was a well established pearl-dealer, well integrated, dealing his business
in the native language – Japanese. Kobe was proud to own a pearl auction, which was a
very important and serious institution till the end of the 1970s. My husband was an
eminent pearl auction member. The auction served its members by giving them a
firsthand product to provide them a first hand knowledge on the quantity and the
output of pearls, which was a very important and major issue to level, to denote and to
brief the prices to bid. It was in fact an exclusivity, mainly to be enjoyed by its
members. My husband was much respected and heard because of his ideas and novelties in the production. He was revered as someone who contributed to the diversification of the pearl business. He offered genuine ideas of enhancing new forms to the
pearls, and introducing new ways of drilling pearls or assessing in colour treatment
and classification. And of course he was acknowledged in his probation and received
many times recognition and acquiescence of the fishermen. All these innovations
were enhanced to ensure and promote pearl creativity more than business activity.

Meanwhile and as a matter of fact to become an auction member in those days was very difficult. Something was also obvious that the auction was a reaching hand to its members, giving them more access and liability to deal and beat the prices on all quality of pearl, which were presented directly from the sources through the fishermen. They were mainly cultured freshwater pearls from Lake Biwa and its surrounding Otsu city. Lake Biwa is situated near Kyoto, the historic capital of Japan's Shogunate era, before Tokyo which later became the capital of the Meiji emperor, till our era. To be an auction member was a privilege, a pride which sometimes rendered members ostentatious!

Pearls are gems by all means, by and by gems have to be revered accordingly, like a queen: comely, aristocratic, noble, fascinating, mysterious, and mostly rare and expensive, the one and only, with the privileges and the homage rendered to that title and reality. And there is no excuse or circumstances that can cross-purpose that reality.

A non-expensive pearl or a wonderfully perfect pearl have the same purpose, the same intention. They were both conceived and implemented with the same sacrifice and technicality and love, the only difference is that the outcome of those pearls could not correspond to the expecting final result or a market asset value.

Henceforth in the 1970s, quality was the target aimed by most dealers. Thus our motto "**Pearls for everyone and for ever**" was born embodying in it a dream, hard work and an ambitious programme to bring forth successful, rewarding, lucrative pursuit of merchandising. It was an assignment of concern, an assessment and a task towards that dream, pearls available and affordable to all! Unfortunately things did not follow that pattern of desired output. The market flooded trivial pearls in big quantity; much of its romance and alluring prestige was being lost. Once considered as the most expensive treasured jewellery of incomparable value in the world, they were gradually being considered almost as accessories, relatively inexpensive decorations to be bought from a big department store, a free market or sold unfortunately on beach, resorts, mixed up with other unworthy commodities, washed up with sand, priced for some miserable tens of dollars in the hands of people who do not know anything about the value of pearl.

There were the permanent dealers, who were residing in Japan, mainly Kobe, who were mostly foreigners like us. Buyers from all over the world would come to Kobe and in an interval of days purchase the pearls. Most of Indian and American buyers would buy in millions. If they had to deal with the Akoya pearls they had to buy directly from the Japanese dealers, who are today incomparable huge names of prestige like

Mikimoto Pearl Company, and many others. On the other hand, in case they wanted to purchase freshwater pearls of all size and quality, they had to buy directly from the auction members, never directly from the fishery, it was a gentlemen agreement that was tightly respected with Japanese. This is why we call them samurai (Japanese knights) respect towards themselves and towards the running business. In one word most of the output of pearls were designated for export. Japanese media, I mean mostly ladies, were not yet ready to enjoy the fruit of their endeavour, nor the blessing of that mysterious and beautiful gem called pearl, Shinju (in Japanese), and it might seem most curious and untruthful that many of them did not even know that their country was a big pearl cultivator and producer. The boom for pearl and jewellery in Japan arrived with their high economy, which opened the door to all dreams, to trips to overseas countries, to seek around after the exclusive and the expensive.

When the Chinese delegation first met my husband on the outskirts of the auction building, prior to that meeting, they had accumulated enough knowledge on his curriculum vitae, especially on his ability and knowledge on the pearl harvesting, and expertise in the culturing procedure of the freshwater pearl, not undermining his knowledge on the different sources and the various quality of pearls: say the South Sea pearls, the cultured Akoya pearl, and some knowledge in his financial strength.

We were very curious regarding their visit, which revealed itself after some self-introduction and unprecedented presentation on the aim and expectations of their trip. I must say I was very proud and thrilled to know later on, about their intention, once they had left our office!

The Wind of Change Was Coming from China

They had come especially to Kobe to meet my husband, to have his idea on the method of pearl cultivation, mainly the freshwater pearl, in order to enhance a better quality pearl with bigger quantity, since in those years, the general output of Japan was not complying to the world's need contrary to some contrasting rumours. The delegation had with them a handful sample of their production, very gently enveloped in a white silk clothing. My husband and I took a close look to the merchandise lying there in that white emasculate soft and caressing wrap. They were pearls indeed, which did not radiate any beauty, neither in their colour nor in their shapes. They were dull, very dull pearls with ivory and brown colours of very small sizes, oddly shaped with crinkle surface. They were either loose or badly drilled and put on string, as the Americans would say rice-on-a-rope. You did not need an expert to see right away there was no way they could compete the Biwa pearls.

My husband's prevalent experiences, his proficiency in the field of his business, made no doubt on his dexterity when it came to appraise the product. He was very discreet and formal. They definitely needed the skilfulness and honest advice in the field, to ensure a better output, to produce pearls of quality and quantity, having in mind that the first pearl farms were already implemented in China as far back as 1968.

After several visits and discussions between the delegation and my husband, they could come finally to terms for co-operation based on tight friendship and honest treatment, a signed contract where my husband, John Alex, was willing to enhance in the sale of tons of pearls coming from their pearl farms. Both parties had to persue one aim, to endorse and promote a better and more bountiful, beautiful pearls. Henceforth my husband's know-how and his contribution promoting to the quality of the Chinese pearls in their quality, sizes and especially forms became the milestone to the growth of the present Chinese pearl industry. We took them around the pearl farms and gave them guidance in their future pearl harvest. They were excited and honoured because of our simplicity and transparency. We did enjoy their attentive and curious attitude, watching and analysing every encounter. Matters of trivial importance were sometimes questionable, friendship flew up effortlessly as if we knew each other a long time ago. Walking side by side with those representatives, I could not have imagined that years after, we too were going to walk side by side on their reefs and shores on the sights of their pearl farms in their homeland. The wind of change had revolutionised and diverted the pearl story towards China, towards its origin.

A Big Responsibility for a Lucrative Marketing

I have a smile while writing these statement, when comparing today's output of beautiful Chinese pearls, so round and thick nacre coated, lustrous and white, with beautiful colours of peach, orange, pink, brown, wine, excelling all kinds of pearls in their category, even surpassing the Japanese pearls in general, including Biwa pearl. What a revolution, what an achievement! Chinese did learn fast and master so well the technique! As for their marketing procedure, a policy needs to be revised. Chinese corporations have the task and the responsibility, since they are controlling the major part of the pearl industry, to assess the respect and enticement due to the pearl that was exonerated since a decade. Pearls are gems, mysterious, elegant, with radiating purity and durability, especially rarity (controlled quantity).

To epitomise the consequences of the pearl story, one has to understand that we were dealing with natural science and human technique. Nature has its time and space to follow up. In regard to the technique and mastery they were to enhance to that natural intelligence. Men indeed were supportive and fully co-active by inducing to the species, in this case the shells or the oysters, but then the animal had to respond to its own natural intelligence. It has to recourse to its own pace in producing the most beautiful secretion that science can ever sense, the "nacre."

To produce better quality pearls, China needed many more decades, bound to more objective realities. Many other facts could explain the objectivity of the matter, pearl culturing could not revolutionise that easily from one day to the other, to bring forth better quality, more quantity was easier comparatively speaking, because it simply needed better technique and mastery. The output could not be ameliorated from one year to the next, it needed more than one decade to start producing pearls which were admitted on the market more or less not rice-shaped and more spherical. With the language of the businessmen, they called them "potato" which needed one more decade to develop to pearls more round and with better lustre, henceforth more attractive.

Efficiency and Performance

China needed two more decades to ameliorate its production and to be counted among the best producers. Only at the end of the 1990s China could produce beautiful and bountiful pearls, thus revolutionising and pivoting pearl marketing towards China. The shapes, lustre, and diversified colours of wine, salmon, white-pink, peach and peach-orange, champagne and brown are unique, often matching original Biwa and even surpassing as higher category pearls. China had won the bet. It needed three decades and a long and tremendously skilled diplomacy, subtle co-operations, and faith to achieve what they have achieved today. Of course, as a matter of fact, many Japanese experts helped them to reach that achievement. Till today many Chinese pearls are still being treated in Japan, including dying and bleaching, and sometimes to emphasize more lustre they have wax like coating to some of their pearls. On the other hand, in China, many new corporations popped up from different prefectures. They organised themselves in culturing and treating conveniently, each competing and trying to conquer the western market which sometimes brought chaotic marketing situation, dumping and devaluating pearl values.

Good Intentions Badly Interpreted

China was enhancing free competition, but that brought insecurity in the business. Initially pearls are not rice for cooking purpose; they are gems. You need rice on a weekly basis, but a woman receives a river of pearl gem once in a life time, mostly at her wedding, or from her lover, effectively if she is still married, she will receive from her husband on different occasions. Not to undermine children or parents who would give or receive depending, as anniversary presents or birthday tokens of love. To that conspicuous happening a woman might eventually add on her personal account a fancy pearl either in size (long) or natural colour pearls (so different, less classical, much more casual and youngish that will suit today's modern lifestyle), the lucrative issue and their attractive prices would encourage the consumer to buy a matching pair of earrings or a diamond ring set with one or two pearls! As for the pearl bracelets, they can wait their turn since a gold one appeals more to ladies, while I wear more than anything a pearl bracelet of freshwater fancy long pearls, very modern and easy to wear that I carry all year round to ensnare me with their peaceful energy. Unfortunately today young women in Europe and America tend to wear artificial pearls, since they can not afford the expensive one. I mean the very big round lustrous pearls or the big long fancy pearls. I have a very good story that happened to me during one of my lectures in Zurich to a big group of international ladies. As I was mentioning the different kinds of pearls with helium-projector and live necklaces that I had carried with me, I had many curious questions on the fancy long pearls since many women did not know about their existence in quantity and since I was insisting on the fact that good quality of pearls are quite expensive, without really giving any arithmetical round up. After the lecture many women rushed to me with their questions, later on approached and took a closer look to the pearls displayed on the table, necklaces and loose pearls of all kinds and all categories. After asking the price of most of the pearls, they took a closer look at a necklace made with fifty fancy long pearls, and one of them timidly added, "I just love these pearls, such a wonder, but I can never dream of getting a necklace made with such big gorgeous pearls, where nature had designed them and technicality had enhance to such enthralled beauty."

"I know," another lady standing next to her went on adding, "it must cost at least one million Swiss Francs (about thirty percent less in Dollars)."

I looked at those women and had a triumphant smile, and told them in a happier and singing tone, "Considering the new cultivation system these pearls are one hundredth times less than their estimation, which does not make them less valuable of course." This is so as explained fully one hour ago in my lecture, thanks to some pioneers and intelligent capable group of foreseers who could make pearls affordable for everyone with their reaching-out prices and quantity to make them necklaces and not only pendants or brooches.

Even the long pearls considered hundreds of years back as pieces of museum today are attainable and could be in one's disposition if the desire is there.

I'd like to remind ladies and gents that pearl is a mystic and spiritual gem. It enhances energy that rarely other gem can, and God knows how much energy a new bride and a groom requires before, during, and after the wedding.

Men too are potential buyers, personally I sold many fancy long pearl pendants and baroque necklaces to male customers, of course they should decide for the right pearl, in this case, mainly fancy long pearls, which would emphasize more and bring forth their male strength (as energy potential) and allure. Do not be amazed since history proves that men, leave aside kings and aristocrats, were the first who appreciated and wore pearls, especially long fancy pearls, which were worn by American natives and Indian warriors.

Some Polemics about the Pearl

The West did not know much about the existence of freshwater pearl till the 1970s. There are few explanation around that polemic since consumers believed that pearls had to be always more round or pinkish-white. Also some reasons attributed to social-economical issues. In another word, they had to acquire more knowledge about the different kinds of pearls, their cultivation and history.

The West came to appreciate freshwater pearls in their integrity for the first time. Around the end of the 1970s, my husband had his roundabout in this meandering acknowledgement. When China flooded the market with big quantity of pearls – as I explained in the prior chapter – they were not the best pearls as seen today on the market. But no matter what shape or colour, they were pearls. Initially, for some time in the eighties, pearls started to be scarce, which made them more demanding. Therefore China restarted to produce more pearls, which brought the price and quality of pearls to a catastrophic situation.

Foreseeing the Future

On the other hand in Japan, till the late 1970s, production from Lake Biwa was still thriving. After the 1980s, production started to diminish, pearl farms were barely surviving, if not altogether closing. This is a disquieting situation, mainly due to pollution from the industries and resort area development. Another major and obvious reason was that the offsprings of those fishermen were not ready to continue their fathers' business. More educated and much richer, they wanted to invest their energy in other adventures. This was a reality that my husband had sensed years back. This reality was another reason to accept and associate his efforts and capacity to a forth-coming future, along with the Chinese corporation. This is how China started to fill the vacuum by producing more and more pearls.

Big Demands Enhanced to the Cultivation of Big Pearls

Until 1987, the average sizes of China's production in freshwater pearls were 2-7 mm. My husband sensed the big demands of special big pearls being seen on the market very rarely; he instructed his fellow operating and cultivating masters to produce pearls of bigger sizes. Round pearls of seven, ten and twelve millimetres and up, also half-drop shapes, round flat button shapes, and coin shapes had a tremendous success on the market. Meanwhile as success generates success, he had an innovative idea to revive the production of very big and long pearls of a few centimetres long. It is very rare to talk of pearl in cm, so we always measure them in millimetre. Already 1cm pearls are more or less scarce and very expensive.

My husband did not give a halt to his long pending dream. In the year 1986, he had a first trial to culture long special big size pearls along with the fishermen in Jiangxi Province. He was enhancing with the expertise of his Japanese friend Hachizume San, who along with my husband gave the "know how" and the mastering technique to this Chinese corporation, to implement pearls of very big size. It was for the first time that China was producing long and extra pearls. They were long pearls of every shape, very lustrous whitish pearls, having a very strong "orient" with the very peculiar sound of gold coins. The market got very excited about these special big pearls. And so some of them were sold 3-4 times higher than one gram of gold.

The history of Fancy (Baroque) Long and Big Pearls

Going back to history, North America was the only source of these categories of large freshwater pearls. It came across in Ohio, Mississippi and Tennessee River basin areas. There is a story which tells that the first discovery of the North American pearl was around the 19th century by a shoemaker, fishing along the coast of New Jersey.

This lucky man caught sight of a large freshwater pearl and since then the American pearl rush was on. For many years, the New Worlds of the Americans along with the pearls that were stumbled upon in the coasts of the Central and South America and the Caribbean, were nicknamed the "Land of Pearls." Most of these pearls were rushed to the European aristocracy, and collected as precious gems. Today some of them are displayed in museums or kept as private collections. Most of these natural freshwater pearls were usually misidentified as saltwater pearls from orient. It is said that the very famous French jeweller Jacques Cartier in the year 1916 bought his store, on New York's prestigious Fifth Avenue, by trading two natural pearl necklaces in exchange of that valuable property. The American industrialisation and overfishing resulted in the depletion of pearl sources. It was revived at the end of the 20th century by a very conspicuous pioneer Mr. Latendresse and his daughter. Those large pearls looked similar to the Chinese fancy long pearls but not as masterful or lustrous as some of the fancy pearls which had a lustre and a moh's hardness of 3.5-4 (measure the hardness of gems), not needing any treatment or bleaching.

Potential Buyers

In India and the Middle East, including Iran and Turkey, there were initial buyers purchasing mostly the output of the Biwa freshwater pearls. They effectively continued to buy the Chinese freshwater pearls. For them pearls could be round, baroque (not round), uneven, rice-shaped, or potato (terms that are used to express pearl forms), not especially white, it could be creamy too; a copy conform to small "natural pearls" or as we call, "Perle Fine", which were initially in shells, muscles, or oysters natural, in all sizes, forms, and colours.

This reality of pearls craving explains the reason why we had so many Indian families living in Kobe, a very important community, whose main activity was mostly to deal with pearls. They had their club too like the Americans, called "The Indian Club", well-off and well-endowed residents, whose memories I cherish. Those friends and business competitors were powerful and intelligent businessmen, having the sense of family and tradition of the hierarchy. They are dignified people living with their conspicuous women and children. I had the privilege to meet Indira Gandhi, the Prime

Minister of India, in their club in Kobe city, and hanker the luck to admire the extraordinary Saris that those Indian ladies were wearing for the occasion. Till today I am dreaming of those beautiful Saris and hoping to have the chance to see once again those opulent designs embodied richness, gold and pearl sawn on silks, some as light and transparent as feather, and some velvety soft and warm.

My love and admiration for the Far Eastern outfits was not fulfilled until much later on, when I discovered the Chinese antique royal outfits, which broadened my insight and admiration towards beauty, grace, creativity and glamour. Asia, what a diversity in richness and glamour!

Indians, too, had to play a big role in the very old pearl history as appreciates and quantity buyers. For them pearls are jewellery to be worn by all women and even men, taking into consideration their rank or caste. In addition, it makes part of their Hindu religion, inscribed in their sacred books and epic tales. Pearls were referred to as a sacred and mystical gem. Another indication and plausible explanation is why their ritual dance performers have to wear jewellery made of gold and pearl. This is why yogis (spiritual, wise men) try to wear pearls with no blemishes, white and not drilled, denoting purity and innocence, enhancing energy of bliss and beatitude. I also read that in their religion (Hinduism) part of the ceremony is the presentation of a not-drilled pearl and its piercing, symbolising their marriage vow!

The Symbol of a Queen

For the West, it is the stone of the month of June. It is a gem that enhances through its unequalled graceful and discrete beauty, an unprecedented comeliness and class to women or to any wearer.

It is a fact that pearl is the most discrete and enthralled gem that you can wear day and night, for a dinner, when playing tennis or going to swim, and when shopping. Apropos its uniform and white colour and especially its baroque (more youthful) shapes of all colour range and grade will never disturb people or make them uneasy. I have worn many times a pearl necklace worth tens of thousands dollars, but never gave the impression that I was being conceited or making a show-off or acting a peacock, bearing in mind that sometimes from remote distance they all look the same. A diamond necklace or a very heavy gold jewellery will undoubtedly attract more attention, giving the impression that you're being ostentatious and flamboyant, especially when you happen to wear in a matinee (day time).

My prevalent experiences in stones are magical, especially with pearls. They radiate compassion, ensuing honesty and transparency in relationship. On a subjective field their unseen waves will enhance love, joy, faith, charity, and sincerity. Also it is a precious gem to promote loyalty and increase fertility; by and large its direct energy will promote youth to the wearer (note therapy with stones in book *Ageless*).

Freshwater Pearls Are Also Queens

One thing I'd like to insist is the fact that talking of pearls' cost and estimate is a most sensitive and controversial issue, especially when dealing with freshwater pearls, which are being subjugated, and attributed officiously a market value not essentially established on to the value of the pearls themselves. Undoubtedly today more than yesterday freshwater pearls are ranking among beautiful pearls, obviously on the market they are not yet expensive, which must not, in no way, enhance to the idea of its quality merge. The contrary is more apparent, it is only a commitment to the management of the product; and it is so much a marketing issue, therefore it is of capital importance not to improvise and hit upon its quality assessment.

As I illustrated with some of my experiences as the wife of a pearl dealer and an expert in the matter, I evaluate and care more about some of the pearl collections today than some of the expensive necklaces I owned in the past; and when I say – I care more, I am alluding to my freshwater pearl necklaces of Chinese origin!

The Birth of a Queen

China was the first nation thousands of years back to introduce the idea and the technique to culture a product from the freshwater mussels. They had the genius for centuries to irritate the freshwater shells to culture them by wooden Buddha (acting as the nucleus) or other religious figurines coated with pearl nacre; they were not pearls but like Mabe pearls (half pearls grown mainly in abalone shells). Figurines covered with pearl nacre stuck to the shell. The real culturing was done hundreds of years later in Japan, in the beginning of the 20th century, in the Island of Mikimoto thus the name of the creator.

Depletion of Thousand Oysters to Price One Pearl

Initially, seas, oceans, rivers and lakes were the ideal places where shell mussels and different types of oysters dwell. These accidental discoveries explain why for centuries men pursued the dream to find these sea-gems which could be found in the body of the mollusc. They became important financial assets and the one who could come across it was blessed with richness and health. The idea was there, but it had to be revived and perfected in Japan at the beginning of the 20th century by Kokuchi Mokimoto, the son of a noodle dealer. In the year 1893 he developed the method of culturing; fist the half pearls on the abalone pearl oysters (Notohahaiotis discus) that were used for culturing of half pearls.

Thus the birth place and the secret of pearl culturing was apprehended on the Mikimoto Pearl Island. The island is also famous for its female divers, "ama" in Japanese. In the old days, as far as recorded history, ama used to brave the ocean at the peril of their lives to find those precious "frozen morning dews" – the pearls in oysters – at the very depth of the ocean. Till today ama performers are diving in the surrounding of Mie prefecture. It is even a tourist attraction. But initially when the cultured pearls were discovered, ama dived to display the baskets of cultured oysters at the depth of the sea which had to grow there at the sea-depth for at least three to four years. To be an ama is a traditional and a very difficult profession. An 18th century painting by Kitagawa Utamaro depicts the story of ama as the mother, the woman, and the beauty, having to brave the dangers of the capricious ocean in order to find pearly-oysters.

The Natural Pearl (Perles Fines)

The natural pearls are formed in the same way as cultured pearls. The only difference in the case of natural pearls is the shell (either in saltwater or freshwater) naturally and accidentally swallows — without human interference — a sharp object or even a parasite, any foreign intruder that the muscle cannot expel. In order to reduce irritation, the mollusc coats the foreign material with *the nacre*, a secretion that it uses to make also the shell-nacre or mother of pearl.

The Cultured Pearls

The seawater-cultured pearls and the freshwater ones are all cultured pearls. They are from different sources and raised in different countries. There are the seawater-cultured pearls such as Akoya pearls and the big size South-Sea pearls and the Black Tahiti pearls thus the name. They are grown on the reefs of Japan, Australia, the Philippines, Tahiti, Indonesia, Burma, Ceylon, Caribbean and Hainan Island (China). Freshwater round pearls and fancy long pearls are grown mainly in China crossing the "Pearl Road", also Japan, North America, especially the long big pearls. As for the Red Sea area, especially Bahrain, you can find some rare natural pearls very exclusive and expensive. And as a rule, it is strictly forbidden to import cultured pearls to those areas or even the method of culturing.

The Freshwater Cultured Pearls

Freshwater pearls grow in freshwater mussel (scientific name *hyriopsis schlegeli*). It has the same procedure as the natural pearl. We call them freshwater pearls because originally they are shells that grow in non-salty water such as lakes and rivers. Unfortunately, in the wild, these mussels are in danger of abolition. Freshwater pearls are tissue-nucleated pearls. The ultimate difference with the natural pearl consists in the way the shell has been irritated, in this case by human interference. There is a special technique of manipulation, which is apprehended in stimulating the muscle. A mastery needs years of experience. In the case of the natural pearls, the process takes place accidentally.

During the culturing operation, the technician opens the mouth of a donor mollusc shell to take its muscle tissue. Next cuts these muscle tissues to small pieces and inserts them into a host, alive shell. This step alone is sufficient to irritate the shell, thus stimulating it to pour the nacre, to start forming a pearl, layer over layer, during an interval of three to four years. This process is very similar to the natural pearls, which forms the nacre to protect itself from the intruder. The freshwater cultured pearl is very similar to natural real pearls since they are entirely nacre, with piled up layers of aragonite. The implemented tissue is there to irritate the pearl to grow, and does not form part of the pearl. The farmers, who before the pearl cultivation were fishermen, lived besides the very famous Biwa Lake, henceforth the name "Biwa pearls" was derived, in the commerce sometimes it is misused while indicating Chinese freshwater pearls; in a way it became a token, a name of prestige to denote good and high quality freshwater pearl.

The Akoya Cultured Pearls

Saltwater cultured pearls have a sphere-cut nucleus and the mantle is implanted in the oyster, to start making a pearl. The sea cultured pearls, also called the Akoya cultured pearls, named after the shell Akoya pearl oysters (scientific name *pinctada furcata*), are cultured mainly in Ise, the Mie Prefecture, where they raise mussels and culture pearls. Mikimoto had succeeded to irritate the oyster by inserting a piece of the oyster's epithelial membrane (lip of the mantle tissue) to a host oyster along with a round nucleus, cut from a U.S. mussel shells, henceforth this sort of nuclei were and still are the basis of all cultured seawater pearls.

Initially nacre is the material that forms all pearls. It is actually composed of two alternating layers of aragonite crystals of calcium carbonate and conchioline, a "non-crystalline binder." These elements are the basis of Amino acid (Amino acids are the building blocks of proteins), eight kinds found in the pearl that the Chinese have been using it in the past and at the present as an alternative medicine. The pearl in powder form is a cure for many sicknesses, especially for the nervous system, to strengthen muscles and many other disorders (see *Ageless*). Many cosmetic firms in Europe and Asia use it in the powder form for cosmetic use (details in *Ageless*).

The natural pearls have many sources and they were revered and appreciated because of being mostly natural, an idea that they gave up gradually, owing to the fact that the quality of the least expensive Chinese freshwater pearls rivals with these natural expensive pearls. I have a nice story on this issue.

On the occasion of our fifth marriage anniversary my husband offered me a new necklace, having given me all categories, except a South-Sea pearl – a pendant of 17 mm with matching earrings and ring and a natural pearl necklace 11 to 13 mm, very round beautiful pearls, although to receive those items I had to wait a few more years and endeavour more in the business.

To excite me with my present, on the day of the anniversary, he had prepared a long speech in a conspicuous way to educate me on the quality of pearls. Patiently I was waiting to open my present! A beautiful pearl box, all in marine-blue colour, contrasting with the pearl lying there gently, on the silken white material. I was happily surprised to see that my pearl had a box; usually I received them in their natural state, without any package or ceremony, a plastic transparent bag handling the problem.

I looked at the pearl necklace, wow! It was truly a natural pearl, the way my husband was explaining. A pearl necklace made of six or seven strings, of 4 to 5 mm pearl-beads, in the tones of champagne to creamy colour. Thinking of the lustre, I must say I was a little bit disappointed, because for me lustre was the first criteria for a nice pearl, then came size, coating, or orient. "Orient" is the name used by dealers to grade or to denote the depth of the nacre, and this is very typical denotation for Chinese freshwater pearls. Having in mind that freshwater pearls are entirely pearl nacre, owing to that they will reflect a distinct rainbow orient. Similarly like diamonds in case when held under a light, they would refract a rainbow-like shine. Unless with Akoya cultured pearls, which reflect very little orient, we can allude of orient to the South-Sea cultured pearls, also to Tahiti pearls, even though they have a nucleus to start their pearling, but owing to their thick nacre coating, they have a very good orient. When light passes around and through its manifold layers, it creates a luminous glow which refracts itself outside the surface of a nice pearl.

I looked at my present again and tried to like it with no pretence, knowing for sure that I had seen, prior to that day, such pearls in kilos in our office. Deep in my heart and somehow through my experienced head, I must admit, not as a pearl dealer's wife but as a woman with subtle experience and taste, my freshwater pearls were much prettier than those natural ones. But I had to abide to the rule of my household than that of the market. My husband, seeing my disappointment, went on adding, "You know Dalita, these pearls are natural pearls, rare, difficult to acquire, henceforth when you sum up the cost, calling onto action the quantity and the output. The market is very sensitive to this reality; therefore calls onto ratio-related facts, accordingly quotes and tugs the prices, in this case high." "They are not treated and they are in their natural colours." Indeed pearls are the only gems that do not need cutting or polishing, they can be worn in their natural state. But of course there too are exceptions to the rule.

That day I wore that natural pearl necklace, and during the coming years only a few times, only to please and revere my husband and sometimes alluding to its high price cost. One thing was sure, I was becoming an integral, unmitigated business woman!

Recently, when I wanted to organise my little treasure box, I saw these pearls nicely wrapped. Having rediscovered, I looked into them for a long time, with a different approach and perspective, the evidence with the eye of an expert, to assess and vindicate my personal treasure. They reflected no enticement, and they did not represent half the price my husband had paid twenty-five years ago. My feminine instinct was right (leave aside expertise), years back when I set forth relinquishing my judgement on assessing the beauty of the pearls. Comparing my necklace to a middle-class non-expensive Chinese freshwater pearl in the market, which could rival the quality of that expensive pearl, or be the equal not in price-value but in their entice-ment and wheedle. What a paradox!

On the other hand, there are big 8 mm to 20 mm size natural pearls round, or drop baroque shapes, that sometimes you have to bet on, at Sotheby's or Christi's auction houses, to acquire them against potential buyers. Since related to their antiquity and history belonging to this or that queen, they are still graded as exclusive pearls, and accordingly sold at colossal prices. Last but not least, there are also the keshi natural pearls, very small 1 mm to 3 mm pearls which in reality are pearl nacres scattered in the mollusc.

Natural pearls are still very exclusive and expensive, depending on the year and the source. Responding to all the criteria of an perfect pearl having to do with the source, lustre, size, purity, colour, and orient. Of course, today on a pragmatic stance, you cannot trade with their relative costs a boat or a house!

history of Pearls

No one knows for sure who were the earliest people to wear or collect pearls. The most expensive and venerate gem, pearls, were introduced to Europe. They were used for decoration and for healing purpose, being natural, rare, and exclusive; in those days it could be worn only by the noble and the rich. A natural pearl necklace was a real treasure of incomparable price, in one word, the most expensive jewellery in the world. Natural pearls were also found in oyster beds in the Persian Gulf, along the coast of India, Ceylon, and in the Red Sea.

Pearls have been mentioned in folklores and epic tales for centuries. Ancient people expressed the reality of pearls in different interesting ways. For example, ancient Egyptians associated pearls with Goddess Isis, a goddess who was a healer and donator of all life. In ancient Rome, pearls were considered the symbol of richness and social standing, a privileged gem only for the Caesars.

As for the Greeks, in mythology they venerated the pearl as the gem that lay the essence of beauty and love, believing that unrivalled beauty was found in its soul. They associated the pearl with the Goddess of Aphrodite who was born of the sea. They believed that when she rose happily from the sea, there were shining droplets that they eventually hardened to become pearls.

The *Bible*, in Old and New Testament, is full of metaphors, alluding to the pearl as being a precious gem; henceforth decorating Icons and religious artifacts, frames of Virgin Mary and Jesus with natural pearls.

Legends with Arabs describe the pearl as being formed when dew drops filled with moonlight, fell into the ocean and were swallowed by shells. Later on ensuing with the Muslim religion, they envisioned the state of bliss to a good doer, and the chosen would be enclosed beneath a tent of pearls. During a marriage ceremony, an Arab as well as an Indian bridegroom has, till today, to bring the bride pearls with many strands, even bunches of pearls, regardless of his financial status; also in the same ceremony the bride has to receive a ruby stone. The pearl is alluring for purity and the ruby stone denoting love. I believe that Arabian and Indian men are very romantic and generous to their brides!

Coming back to Italy of the Middle Ages, the Renaissance period, where artists expressed in many paintings their love for the pearl. A very famous artist of his time, Botticelli, drew a famous canvas "The Birth of Venus" (1484-1486) using the idea of Greek mythology. Venus, the goddess of love, was born from the shell in the sea. The canvas represents a beautiful naked maiden washed up in a shell coming out from the sea on the legendary island of Cythera. The canvas represents a Madonna face, of grace and beauty, with a gaze full of melancholy. It goes on showing Venus standing in a big shell. She is the embodiment of pure innocent love, covering her nakedness with her hair and hands. According to the mythological tradition, the Greek god took his revenge on his cruel father Uranus by castrating him and throwing his genitals into the sea. Their combination with the foam of the sea and the shell brought forth the goddess of love, Venus. So the concept of a beautiful woman is an allotment to an alluring and enthralling pearl.

In England, stretching back from Middle Ages till today, pearls were worn by the aristocracy as well as the plebeian. It was the ultimate gem for kings and queens and was considered an exclusive privilege of a royalty. Around the 17th century, the Duke of Saxon made a decree prohibiting the wearing of pearls for the nobility, professors, and doctors, thereby restricting their use only to the royal court. Elisabeth I of England had an avidity and ravenousness for pearls. She used to receive pearls from the New Continent, prevailed on and fetched by his army generals, the conquistadors. Portraits of her showed the queen wearing dresses encrusted with pearls and wardrobes of earrings, necklaces, bracelets, pendants, and tiaras. She even wore pearls in her hair, gowns and slippers.

In the Georgian and Victorian periods, pearls were worn in a more symbolic way. It was used as morning jewellery, to symbolise the tears of affliction and faith. The British loved pearls very much, which had been substantiated and evinced by their heads of state Queen Elisabeth II as well as the late Princess Diana. They loved pearl and wore it as much as possible, discerning her back the title she deserves.

China is the unique example that not only venerated pearls as a precious gem but found the ways to venerate the gods through their discovery of relic pearling. We do not know exactly when started the pearling of these relics and who had the initial idea of irritating the shell for pearling, most probably the Buddhist monks. Most of the emperors were fascinated by these pearly relics. Many antique drawings show Chinese emperors and rulers wearing pearls and palaces decorated with that rare gem. Stretching as far as the Han Dynasty (206BC-AC220) which had reached, according to accurate records, a high cultural and educational standard, adopting Confucianism as their religious path, it became more organised thus implemented the basis of high and strong Empire of China. The pearl was also seen in the Tang, Song, and especially the Ming dynasties, as well as on the threshold of the 20th century with the Manchu or Qing era and many drawings showing Empress Cixi wearing pearl necklaces. Initially to own a nice collection of pearl by a person was to denote the esteem and rank of that person.

Unfortunately today pearls have lost their extensive value. On the other hand, on a pragmatic level, cultured pearls have filled the gap of the natural pearls which are more accessible considering cost, quality and quantity, not undermining the source of the pearl that could eventually evaluate its market value.

There is another assessment about pearls – they are living gems. Henceforth we have to give special care to them by wearing them as much as possible. They live with our warmth and physical touch, and feel our emotions at the fondling of our skin. And just like the skin of our body, they do not like pollution, they do not like chemicals, nor be impinged upon with excess. Even too much our blessed sunshine is disquieting for them. It is a mutual care between the pearl and you – the more you take care of it, the better it will enhance you with its palpating beauty and its healing energy. All my life I wear pearls, I must have them on me everyday, as earrings or a necklace or mostly a bracelet as an energy carrier. I also eat them, in the form of powder; of course I learned in China about their medical alternative inducement to health. They keep me young and healthy. Initially I also make cosmetic creams too. I use pearl powder in my creams and soaps and believe me, they are wonderful (more in "About health and beauty" in *Ageless*). A great paradox of the pearl story is that the least expensive freshwater pearls in the market challenges to be a match for and come up to be compared quality-wise, with expensive natural pearls, since it is very difficult to differentiate them with the naked eye, especially the freshwater cultured pearls, the ones that are not bleached.

I have another story relating to this reality of natural pearls bearing comparison with the freshwater pearls. End-1980s I visited Russia with my husband. In Moscow, we had a few free days to make a tour. Therefore, according to our schedule, we had, among many other places, to visit the Kremlin and the Red Square. It is exciting that I was visiting all the places that had inspired Tolstoy, Dostoyevsky, Pushkin, Pasternak, and the great composers like Tchaikovsky. What a day I was thinking, and felt so lucky. Of course Saint Petersburg was more inspiring with its gorgeous churches and palaces, but it was in Moscow that I saw Kremlin's most prestigious legacy, a bequest so proudly displayed the family jewellery of kings and queens, the reminiscence of the fabulous collection of Empress Catharine the Great, a royal gown which belonged to her richly embroidered with pearls, hardly exposing any part of the fabric. What a lavishing sight denoting richness and power! Of course there were many other exquisite and attractive things, breath-taking objects, full of art and craft, a richness of inestimable value, a patrimony of the nation, an endowment of pride enhanced through unknown individuals, who had contributed to that wonderful exhibit.

I saw all the beautiful armchairs encrusted with precious stones and pearls and embroidered sets of royal caps and gowns, with natural antique pearls. The piece that impressed me belonged to Tsarina Catharine the Great of Russia (1729-1796). There are other decorations: gowns, crowns, and horse saddles decorated with precious stones and antique pearls.

I stood in front of a red velvety cap embroidered with very fine, small, natural pearls of 2 to 4 mm. They could have been only natural pearls, taking into account the period it denoted, the 18th century. The pearls had a dark beige to ivory colours, and not so lustrous. The cap's red colour was almost impossible to see, out of the enticed pearls on the material, unless from the back side. Effectively it must have been very heavy to wear, I ratify, covered with so many pearls, undeniably so royal and so glamorous. There is the tremendous unimaginable human sacrifice, having in mind the sequel of the human souls involved in the achievement. An artist (I was told that day) had lost her sight, after finishing embroidering that scarlet cap. What an assessment, a hard-core effort for a queen's lasciviousness, endorsing her power to hanker after her royal desire to acquire such royal pieces.

Beyond any doubt, cultured freshwater pearls of Chinese origin could match, thus rival those antique pearls, giving evidence and invoking the same outlook and bearing witness of their quality and grading. To epitomise my concern, I jumped to the conclusion that the Tsarina would have eulogised and hankered after the new millennium Chinese cultured pearls.

Hailing China

O ur journeys, voyages and hectic trips were well apprehended and perceived. Year after year we cross the other continent to that faraway land, so different yet so attractive and compelling. There is an unusual distinction which did not have any hostility in its unlikeness and singularity and a divergence which would not leave you indifferent there. What a big land I was thinking! During my frequent trips I have been from East to West, crossing the North to the South, but I have done only some part of the land, even though I had made the major cities, the major capitals, political as well as financial ones. I had travelled to the inner lands from the famous to the smaller cities, but again I cannot say today for sure that I have seen half of China, at least that's my feeling, because at each visit I hear new names, new spots to visit; it is an endless voyage. Such a big land, a world in itself, a continent that needs one's whole life to be overhauled because compared to other lands or countries there is always a diversification. You are constantly brought up with different scenes, different customs and behaviour, and creativity, not to undermine the different dialect of each province and city. I came to realise through the years after so many attempts to learn the dialects that they were quite different from the Mandarin – the main language the government expresses with. On an objective stance, I do have the satisfaction of having visited the most outstanding cities or let's say the pre-eminent cities which have led China historically, financially, economically, and sociologically. I still recall the attitude of the people on the streets which manifested a general emphatic feeling of pride, to belong to a great nation, a general consciousness that was well revealed and asseverated in almost every Chinese I met. They knew effectively they were the offspring of a nation which had contributed, in his past history so much to humanity.

My next remembrance towards their general attitude was their impartial and open-minded view on their superiority in number and their proliferation. I was well aware of the important and unambiguous role they will play in our future and posterity and that unequivocal definite role will be of capital importance for the balance of our world. How on earth were they going to manage with the words Occident and Orient, East and West? So many different ideologies were being on stake, an imperious and valorous venture which had to be encountered by China to maintain a just and prosperous future for all. Of course all these issues had some impact on our past and present adventures and dealing. Even though they were not attributed directly to us, nonetheless on a pragmatic and matter-of-fact stance, they had a big impact on some of our decisions and itineraries regarding our business endeavours.

I was telling myself that a great nation has got a big responsibility in his decisions no matter what. This is how we recognise, perceive, and respect a great nation. Summing up my impressions on China after so many years of tight relation, I have sensed and perceived their subtle and nimble stance, their insight and perception embodied thousands of years of political and social experience, a long-term awareness which heightened in me a tranquil feeling of gratification. China is a peaceful and generous nation I went on meditating, a country who is ready to welcome the others, the difference too, indiscriminately and arbitrarily apprehended. They were ready to synergize their forces and implement a modern nation at the service of humanity, and mostly to their outnumbered population. I do not think today's China has the feeling to impose its civilization as the superior one as it was their old belief, which kept their empires immobile and caused stagnation cut off the reality of the other European empires which were running towards high technique and modernisation. Of course China today is a country with different insight, he embraces another approach, a new millennium that projects towards a balanced tacit and concrete objectiveness. This nation inspires the people in the street, embracing an openness towards the outside world. Once these words reverberated in my mind, I had a smile, thinking how on each visit my husband and I were witnessing the tremendous change in their inner system which reflected themselves in their comportment, in their outfit. Looking around the outstanding changes in the cities that I saw flourishing year after year, changes that stood for thousand words, I was thinking, what a tremendous pace from the day I visited them the first time till today at the threshold of the 21st century!

Affirming Its Rank Siding the Big Nations

While I was writing these pages, China was once again appointed and was under the spotlight of the news media of the world. It was alluring to its unbelievable success launching their first man-loaded rocket. The world was flabbergasted seeing China has proved itself once again, by reaching the stars, this time not by transcending through the mind and spirit, but through highest space technology. The world was stunned and overwhelmed, welcomed the newcomer for the long and arduous voyage to the universe. On October 15, 2003, China launched for the first time in history a man-loaded rocket, in the desert of Gobi, carrying a "Taikonaute", Yang Liwei. The adventure of the big voyages to the stars of the new millennium had started. A new hero was born for a new era, a son to be proud of, the whole nation was claiming his new star, who before landing safely in inner Mongolia, had to turn around "the blue planet" – the Earth – fourteen times in an interval of twenty-one hour. This is a programme of exploration which needs all measures and grants, all out of scientific and technical intelligence with a balanced and rather low cost. This new venture will contribute to the people of China a new aspect, a new confidence. This voyage insured China the allotment to be engaged to the new era of space programme, henceforth committed to become the third nation in the rank of explorers of the space race.

harnessing Nature to Recall

The singing of birds around my windowpane diverted my thoughts to their direction. I suddenly realised that some moment had elapsed. I raised my head to watch the source of the gleaming warm light incessantly hitting my face. The strong caress of the beam coming from the sky was like a cosmic ribbon on my head and an infinite inspiration to my heart. I tried to blink the sun, which was now so high up in a clear blue sky, shining in an orange-pink fiery outfit, majestic as ever, standing there timely and in all its power. There was nothing to stand on his way, nothing to disturb this charming moment between the celestial love and me, a moment to be remembered and that's what impelled me to inscribe that admirable fraction of a moment in time. I took a long breath as if to be sure if I was still breathing the fresh air of

Switzerland or rather Zurich and not that of China. I was so far away with the state of enticement and lure that for a moment, I was propelled and carried away through the impel of the singing of birds and the soft air on my face, inundated with the heat of the sunrays once again enveloping all my being.

I went on enumerating my aftermath, realising that my husband and I had devoted more than a quarter of a century at the pursuit of our pearl business. Actually thinking back, it was the main reason and purpose of our trips which brought us in contact with China.

A whole life in an adult's itinerary is at the service of a business, which had to become a goal, an ambition to realise and bring forward a historically delineated business and to walk on its blueprints.

Pearl story was and is a Chinese story, and is the story of people who ever wanted to enhance towards that end to contribute to its growth as a business trend, project and line, thus enhancing and reviving its long-time history. My husband was a pioneer in this project and purpose. His endeavour was an effort aiming to help mother nature (mother of pearl), reaching her a hand thus contributing and enhancing her in bearing "the Pearls", to bring forth bountiful and diversified pearls of different sizes, colours, and shapes (ref. to book *Ageless*). Pearls, the nature's miracle, were conceived in oysters of different species at the bottom of lakes, seas, and rivers.

I will try to recall events and situations which will inform about the character of the native people, to recall big writers, missionaries, and businessmen, who have visited, lived, and are still living in China, having experienced what I also experienced and apprehended through my unprecedented narration, recounting with the people of another world and of another dimension.

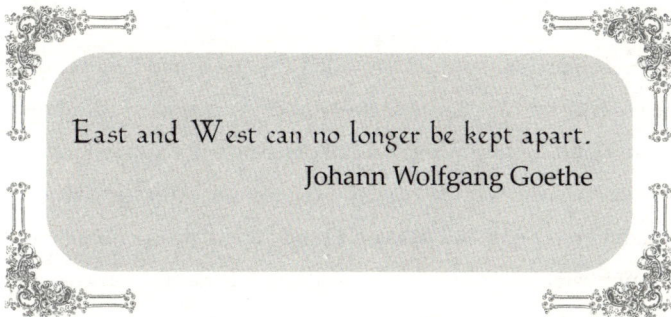

> East and West can no longer be kept apart.
> Johann Wolfgang Goethe

Ancient Ruins, Modern Cities:
China in the 1970s

China is an old culture moving into the 21st century, a land of many contrast: urban and rural inhabitants. To understand China and the Chinese, one has to discover its past history and understand its political and social values. It needed two revolutions in the 20th century to put China on the path of modernity. The present is mounting like a pagoda year after year. I wonder and am curious about its future yet to come with many surprises, owing to the unpredictable and subtle Chinese character.

In 1979, while we were there, direct foreign investment was introduced after a ban of thirty years and four areas in Guangdong and Fujian were designated as special economical zones, to create new opportunities in establishing joint ventures and to promote export-oriented industries.

Of course China's economic policy did not stop there, since the mid-1980s more than fourteen major coastal cities and other coastal areas were opened to foreign businessmen and investors, to enhance modern technology and modern initiatives to the country.

All these events and situations had one-sided advantage and benefited mostly to the Chinese. The government was endorsing new policies, deterrent measures, new regulation to eradicate confusion and irregularity especially through the policy of some Chinese corporations, who wanted to get on the top very quickly. The gate opened slowly and steadily to achieve and develop a modern and prosperous economy. On the other hand, notwithstanding the Occident was eager to explore and experience the traditional Oriental ideas, inventions and contribution in philosophy, art, culture, and science which are as important and conspicuous as advanced technology which are rewarding only for some areas in life.

Our world is populated of so many nations, around 200 or so, and so many ethnic groups with different languages and religious beliefs. But as human souls there is a strong connection among us all. We have been created of the same way and will pass away one day. So what prevails is the consideration and respect towards those people that we encounter on our way either as tourist or through business, also on cultural and economical ventures. Then of course there is always this indifference or ostentatious behaviours, whose stem is born from ignorance, or ego-based, coming to meet the difference, which in reality paves the way to new curiosity and knowledge. I can grasp now the major reasons of our history and geography courses at school; that had to act as precursors to those different cultures. On a pragmatic issue I was conveyed to encounter and itinerate my conclusive and rational inducement towards the new, the different and the unknown.

To depict about the Chinese cultural itinerary, not undermining their glorious past, brought me very close to their aspiration and feelings; this big land, where principles were tight but actions were taken to more openness, less repressive.

All my life I have been living in small countries of about 3-6 million population. Nations who had also a past and present history, but their story is like the story of a nightingale, while the story of the Chinese and their awakening is like the dragon who slept for some hundred years, since then China is awake and resolute. Modern leaders had drawn and setup the sketch of the glorious China coming out of his ruins, supporting a firm and strong basement for China, to step up without fear since they were great builders and foreseers.

People's character do not change, they only adapt to the times and givens. I might be wrong, but that's how I understood of my lifelong experiences about people and their undertaking, the issues of the past, the present, and the forthcoming future.

In the Ming Imperial Palace in Nanjing, Jiangsu Province. I was wearing an antique precious gown of an Aristocrat of the Qing Dynasty.

In the Ming Gugong, imperial palace of the Ming Dynasty until 1421. I was wearing the precious antique gown of a princess of Ming period, the same gown as the scroll behind showing the princess.

The sight of pearl harvest in Poyang Lake in Jingdezhen, Jiangxi Province.

Hainan Island. The small fishery boat used to ram on the lakes by the fishermen to inspect the pearl shells and to carry them on the shore when the time of harvest has come.

John (my husband) in his office in Monthey, Switzerland, with a Shanghai delegation on a visit, appraising together the rewarding quality of freshwater pearls.

At the shore of the Poyang Lake in Jingdezhen, Jiangxi Province, with the head office managers .

A pearl factory Joint venture in Suzhou, Jiangsu Province, a pearl city with canals and most splendid gardens near Shanghai. The Chinese apprentice and I were sharing our knowledge and vision on the rebirth of pearl industry.

The picture shows a huge pearl factory in Nanjing, Jiangsu Province. Talented Chinese young women, attentive and hard workers, were listening to the suggestion of my husband, and I was the ultimate substantiate student and admirer.

Beijing, my love. John and I were on the path of historic and majestic capital in the famous Tian'anmen Square.

In front of one of the pavilions in the Forbidden City, Beijing. Behind the ornate door with golden and orange decorations was where the last emperor, Pu Yi, used reside.

The family: with our son, Arthur, and two daughters, Dalia and Alexia, in the Summer Palace in Beijing built for the Dowager Empress Cixi, in the ornate corridor surrounded by superb pavilions and gardens and the most amazing marble boat in the Kunming Lake.

My husband, John, with his young daughters in Nanjing, Jiangsu Province, in a pavillion in Lake Mochou.

SECTION TWO

The Entrance Door
Was Hong Kong

The first time I visited China was in 1973 along with my husband. That was of a very short stay. It was only a visit of three days on the borderline of Mainland China with Hong Kong. Needless to say it was business-oriented and was my first visit to Mainland China. I was more excited about the trip than the idea of seeing a new land, I was still living in Japan and I was yet under its spell, its Far Eastern charm and reality. I must admit I did not see much of China. I had the impression to enter a small door opened from a huge gate and we had to come in and out. On the other side of the door, people in uniform were waiting for us very cordially and inquisitively!

1976 was my real trip to Mainland China, along with my husband, my mother and my three children. We always stayed first in Hong Kong to be able to continue to Mainland China, wherever we were planning to go.

I was fascinated also by Hong Kong. Hong Kong city is divided to two major sections or cities. The Hong Kong side is more dense and active; in a certain way playing the heart of the city, with its shopping centres and offices, its international bureaux and offices.

The Kawloon side has more residential area, with its beautiful hotels and exquisite restaurants and night clubs, not to forget its piled shopping centres so dense and full of all kinds of goods, say, from ivory shops to film shops, merchants of various commodities, clothing and beauty shops, not to forget the arcades and the moles, the fish markets and food, herbal and grocery markets, mainly found in the Chinese zone of the city.

Omnipotent

1976 was the beginning yet of another adventure which was to change all my concept and standout towards social welfare and an attribute of harmony and co-existence. I had to discover China and its people. The whole family was there, including my mother who had visited us in Japan, henceforth we proposed her to continue her trip with us to Hong Kong and Mainland China. This was a very good occasion to look-in continuing her sightseeing to the extreme Orient. As for me this was a good opportunity, a propitious moment to enjoy the presence of my mother many more days, meanwhile giving her the joy to discover along with us this historic new land. We flew to Hong Kong first, and stayed there for about one month to continue our main and scheduled trip to Mainland China.

Since we were intending to stay for an undetermined period of time, we had reserved a suite from a four star hotel. Henceforth our stay was one of its kinds. My family almost completed. The presence of my mother with us was another gratification. It gave me a notion of accomplishment, a satisfaction, in the relation of a child to her parent, an adored opportunity to see a mother sharing happy moments.

My mother had always lamented my departure to the Extreme Orient, to Japan, as a new bride, leaving family, big circle of friends behind, establishing a life in Kobe, Japan, away from my loved ones. There's no need to assert that the feeling of completeness before this unprecedented arrangement was of big joy.

You did not have to act or to prepare yourself to be happy in Hong Kong, since the boisterous city was a charming and happy place in itself. The brouhaha of the day time and the illuminated city by night could not give way to melancholy, or any disappointment; every body was busy. The city was boiling with activity and we were taken in a kind of a whirlpool where everything, all kinds of ingredients, rejected and injected. The air was being dispersed with the acre smell of food, raw or cooked, blended together with exotic and queer perfumes, smell of singular, weird, and meantime marvellous merchandises were displayed in the aligned dense boutiques.

The ferry that we used to take to cross the city from Kowloon to Hong Kong was something that enchanted my children, because there at least was free air circulating from one reeve to the other, whirling and pirouetting was a merry-go-round. The sound of the soapy water was an enchanting lullaby, to appease their exhausted body.

Opulence, pulchritude extravagance, noise, smell, dust, people jammed everywhere, trash on the side of the pavement; accomplishing the picture of the city in those days which looked like a drawing of surrealist paintings of early 20th century, where philosophy and fervent poetry were the expression of duality between the objective, the apparent, the tangible and the colourful. Ideas and feelings took shapes and colour on the canvas of renowned painters such as Miró, Tanguy, Ernst, and Salvador Dali. Surrealist sculptures such as Giacometti had their contribution expressing the abstract, the subjective, the deep thought of the innovative and revolted mind. The surrealism era in Europe was a revolution in art, an art whose repercussions were felt everywhere on every field for a few decades. Like all forms of art from the romantic era to the impressionist, the surrealism are from abstract to cubism.

Hong Kong was an ephemeral surrealistic painting for me, so much contrast, so many alluring symbols, the old and the new. All these extremes made the charm and inexplicable success and beauty of Hong Kong, an old city, a most modern, reputable, extravagant city, who became part of Chinese sovereignty in the year 1997.

All of these memories shot coveted the family photo that I had to bring back home with me. The enchanting memories of a life time, a treasure and a richness that did not need a special place to hide unless in your mind.

Of course Hong Kong city did make part of my treasured memories, being remarkable in my lifelong history, when first I landed on a Far Eastern territory for my honeymoon and later on many times making a gateway between Japan, China and Europe. We cannot undermine its history and the role it played when East encounters West. Hong Kong was and still is the big door to China, the mouth of Asia and the purse and the pulse of the world.

But, as I said, for me the importance of the city is more sentimental than economical. Hong Kong embodied many memories, he saw me getting more mature and changing concepts and insight, regarding and treasuring the old and appreciating the new under different light, perceiving and recognising facts with the morality of the times and givens.

Between our adventures are sight seeing of countryside with its Victorian mansions of the island and exploring cultural tours, visits to the museums as well as its very famous "Aberdeen" – the boat restaurant – where very famous and less famous figures of our world stars of the cinema, crowned heads, big authors, and politicians had visited. We could see their photos on the wall, pictures with their signaturess and some words of their appreciation, for the excellent culinary display. I must underline that Hong Kong is famous for its magnificent restaurants, for every taste and every budget. Different cuisine from Cantonese to Sichuan, Italian to very refined French cuisine, not to forget all the other different culinary presence through ethnic groups, who could identify and substantiate their presence with their culinary art. The places that I loved to walk most, was when I took a tour visiting the showcases of the shops, in the very famous Cameron road, from west to east, to Chatham and Tsim Sha Tsui roads, a window-shopping which would leave you in wonder and fascination. All these were so easy to like once you are sure of this place, nothing could retain you from liking this enchanting, happy, lively city. It was a woman's paradise indeed, but for me, besides being attractive, it became memorable and significant, encountering an episode that I lived through, an event that I still recall after so many years.

As I said earlier, Hong Kong is a big city, one of the most populated cities in the world on an account per square meter. So who says big city can think of the constrains to all kinds of events, the strange, the good, and the bad! If you happen to forget a package in a popular place, be sure after a few minutes it is vanished, executed by professionals you can not even prove or appoint the thieve, even if you have an idea of the executor; there may be curious persons who wanted to know the content of your shopping!

There was another prejudice which used to circulate through the streets of Hong Kong in regard to the naughty doers. You call this prejudice or conspiracy or discriminative speculation, the poor being pinpointed as erroneous doers since the logic of the rich and abundance surpassing their thought. In the mist of plenty it is too challenging and appetizing to be high on the gear, an abundance of indescribable measure.

"What Goes Around Comes Around"

A Rich Man in hong Kong

What will follow in my story will show that we should not haste in our judgements and to be blurred with an outweighed prejudice to a point to make us blind and ignorant, not acting as impartial and upright towards those issues. Beauty and abundance are compelling and attractive, tempting to the rich as well as to the poor, but fortunately the government, civil and penal laws, education, religion and philosophy come to the rescue of the human character, to cut short a devastating appetite of owning too much. Or the other way, in case of not having, being deprived of the plenty, help to find complacency, contentment and pride on other fields of life, to distract the soul with more non-materialistic richness which is the essence of our being, a concept, a conviction of life, an appraisal of different values, for the ones who were eager to grasp, or have experienced the meaning of that kind of introspective and inward-looking assessments.

Well, in that overpopulated Hong Kong, I had to meet such a person, who was living on another dimension, a person at ease and in contempt of his own achievements which he accumulated all along his life and have heightened in him the feeling of fulfillment. This man was one of the richest and vibrant men in Hong Kong. I recall my protagonist after so many years, prerogative to the consecutive and apparent events that took place during our stay in Hong Kong. The Old Testament tells us the story of Sodom and Comoro, two corrupt cities, whose denizens were pagan, not willing to abide by God's commandments, yet lavishly living and abusing on material. Therefore,

God chose to save one righteous couple among the inhabitants of the cities. My protagonist, in this case "the rich man of Hong Kong", did somehow rescue his city to safeguard its reputation, thus proving undeniably that there are always undeceived characters, satiated souls, spirits that are satisfied with their own endeavours, and regarding the brouhaha of the outside world as an illusionary momentary happiness to be enjoyed acceptably, up to the mark, thus easy in his mind and soul.

What will follow is my recollection and impressions of our unassailable long stay in Hotel Hong Kong, which was situated in one of the busiest streets of Hong Kong city. There were stuffs florid and aureate, resplendent the best and richest merchandises from all over the world; leave aside and not taking into account the Asian world, which is a world in itself. Hong Kong is a city – as my late father would have expressed – where you can find even the "lion's milk" and that could be taken as true statement, taken into account and considering the presence of lions in the nearby jungles of Korea, Thailand, the Philippines and all the other neighbouring countries. What will follow next is the authentic story of the "richest man in Hong Kong."

He was a Chinese man from Guangdong Province. He fled away from China during the civil war, leaving behind his family: father, mother, and siblings. He had married a girl of his province, a healthy, pretty, hardworking, and docile woman, who had given him two children. They had an insecure life full of turmoil, therefore the dream of another land of another horizon was imminent. A life with new beginnings was so compelling for him that he could see only the positive side of the givens, not realising that he should not leave his two children back in the country, who were meanwhile married, each having their own children.

His wife had great difficulty to assimilate her new life. She was missing her kindred, the blossom of their fruits, despite the fact that she had new branches on her family tree. She had not seen the new members of the family born, a privilege that she qualified, an opportunity of unequal treasure. She missed also her landscapes back home, the infinite lands of green meadows, the smell of the red earth on which she was raised and nourished; all her happiness and misery rose from those fields, fields that carried her aspirations and toil. That earth was her blessing, her source of strength. She was nourished by its heat, its abundant rain, and fury of its storms. She regretted their erroneous thinking and decision for having chosen the path of immigration. She believed that to consolidate new givens and situation in life one needed more energy, inspiration, and will. She lacked that energy. She believed her new venture brought confusion in her life, since entering in the realm of the unknown thus contemplating and feeling the new forces, which if not handled properly would lead her to desolation. She was well aware that her life was bound tight to her family and her simple habitation – built on the outskirts of her village – those were her absolute richness. Despite her correct and decisive actions and demeanour, she could not compensate their equal, in that lavish, frivolous, happy city of light and heat.

Mr. Shu Shin Hua was a man in his late sixties, a small man with a healthy and vigorous corpulence on an amazingly skinny body. He was still very Chinese; this was my way of analysing the different aspects of Chinese that time, in one word, very traditional in his outfit and in his outstanding behaviour. I met him during my stay in Hong Kong. All day long he used to wear his Chinese black cap with colourful flowers and a pustule hanging from the middle of the cap. All the time we were there, and on each occasional meeting, he had his white and bright yellow jacket ornate with very delicate Chinese design, with matching delicate cotton black trousers. Very seldom we saw him wearing his Sunday outfit of a very exclusive black silk, with colourful designs on the back and front part of the sleeves of his jacket. Of course today things are so different, since I am talking of my encounters some three decades ago when Chinese outfits were not that familiar to the general public. These models inspired many big contemporary French and Italian designers.

From time to time he, too, used to speak to us of his own children, especially his grand children, having missed them, and the regret for not having seen them getting bigger, since he used to add that nature had blessed his offsprings. His children were lucky to bear two male babies each, and this had its capital importance for him. First male babies were always revered in the East regarding social acceptance and a concept as old as history. Second during the regime in the 1970s, according to the population policy, one is encouraged to start to marry not early and bear one child, a very strict birth control. Henceforth these issues explained the special interest and attachment of Mr. Shu Shin Hua to my family. I reminded him of his young daughter and my children a parallel resemblance with his grand children! As for my mom, till today I am not sure if she suited in his picture, since in no way could she have reminded him of his wife, since my mother was a very young-looking, modern and healthy woman, having no affinity for the old Chinese perspective or for the new. She had a big difficulty assimilating herself to this Oriental city. Thanks God! Hong Kong was the modern version of the other cities she had to visit, or else our stay would have turned to be a real catastrophe.

We had been prolonging our stay because of our business. We, my mother and my children, had complaints, as it is with visitors in general. We were starting to feel squeezed in that hotel room on the eighth floor. Despite the fact that we had enough rooms to make us feel rather comfortable, nothing could replace the comfort of a house and the freedom with which our children would react. My mother started complaining and counting the days. As for my children, they never had enough time to go out for sightseeing. They were willing to walk in the heat of the day from one street to the other, visiting all the nice playgrounds, to end up regretting their desire, whereby undermining my lectures and the explanations about the hot and humid weather and the physical exhaustion, and with it some flu or any undesirable physical discomfort, of which I was terribly cautious and wary. Yet once questioned about the programme of the day, they would indulge and give predilection and choose to do promenades rather than to stay in the cramped area of our hotel suite. I taught them all the songs that I had in my repertoire as all mothers, I guess. My son was giving signs of big fondness at math, natural sciences, and history. As for my daughters, they were acting as future painters. There remained not a space on the walls of our hotel room that did not have their drawings which gave them even more happiness and encouraged their young and innocent souls to draw more of their impressions of their encounters and events in Hong Kong and its surrounding.

On Our Way to Guangzhou

Guangzhou was not very far from Hong Kong, so we did not need to dine in the train.

After a while, my husband asked me why I was not wearing my diamond ring.

I replied very tranquilly that it was in the bag with all the other jewels that I gave to mother to take care, while I was preparing our departure, and then of course I did not recuperate it back, and it is always with mother.

Then I turned around to my mom, who was playing with my daughters.

"Mother, where is the purse I gave you this morning at the hotel, before we went down for breakfast?" For a while there was a silence. As an answer mother stopped playing, turned around, and made some gestures to stand up and reach to her handbag, which was arranged on the shelf besides the other big suitcases. My husband jumped right away from his place to help her with it. Now I was very impatient to get my purse, in order to put on my ring, to hanker after my husband's will.

My husband

He always yearned to see me happy and content, a heed that made him proud and satisfied without becoming ostentatious. He was an overt generous man, even-tempered and composed. He wanted to see me wearing jewels that he had generously offered: beautiful necklaces of precious stones and earrings and matching bracelets, not to mention the pearls I owned of all categories. Of course I was not very keen on wearing them, constraint to become an attraction. Being young I was rather timid and reserved. His successful life and prosperous financial situation came up to expectations, and complied with his dreams. I was the rose of his bouquet and our offsprings the adjacent buds, which manifested the accomplishment and embellishment of that bouquet.

My husband had worked hard to his own success. Deserved every penny he had earned through sweat and hardship. He had a very special karma. This man in his late thirties was an Armenian, charismatic guy, who was encountering the Far Eastern countries on his account, without the help of any second or third party. He had decided on projecting his endeavours through an itinerary that he had designed and discovered all by himself, as a legacy conveyed to him from a very adventurous father, thus like father like son, hailing the seas and crossing mountains intrepid, brave, and resolute.

Before he had met me, he had already discovered his Silk Road or the road scattered with pearls. He not only bought pearls, but also knew how to deal with them once they were out of their mother of pearly-oyster. He knew how to disguise their impurity or enhance their beauty to bring forth their market value, exalt and embellish women. Pearls are the most natural tokens of our nature, delicate, smooth, and lustrous, yet hard and impervious; effectively to resist the bite of a suspicious tradesman's teeth, who wants to make sure or proof against her authenticity, had to undergo this kind of treatment that is biting through the pearl! Fortunately this is not a practice done by all pearl tradesmen! A professional eye has other methods to decide the pearl's criteria: the natural one from the fake, a bad from a good, lustre from dull, rosy colour from whitish hue. This is a profession which needed a lot of patience and years of experience, to reach to a fulfilling expertise in the line of pearl business. Things did not stop only to the commerce of the pearl. The market's demands were getting bigger, so my husband, along with his fellow Chinese from different provinces and corporations, were trying to study the way to promote the quality and the quantity of the pearls. Huge programs were undertaken to bring forth different sizes, different shapes, and colours of pearls. The pearl industry was being established in China, and my husband was a pioneer in the event and accomplishment. He was not the only Armenian pioneer of his lineage, others have crossed and lived on the Chinese territory. Centuries back there were many other Armenians who had tried to establish commercial relations or other issues either on a private ground or as an emissary sent through governments. There were many intrepid and intransigent Armenians who had walked and chased the Silk Road, much before Marco Polo undertook to itinerant on those roads. They crossed all the way from east of the Caucasus and entered the Chinese territory, contingent to pay tribute to the big land and its inventive conspicuous people to boost, exchange and enhance commerce, science, and astronomy. The legacy of this very small republic of Armenia and the determination of its survival in the past as well as in the present is of capital importance. Today it's a small enclave neighbouring on the north Iran, on the west Turkey, to the east Azerbaijan, and Georgia to the north. Just before the end of the 20th century, at the collapse of the former Soviet Union, Armenians could enjoy an independent state so much dreamt and urged almost by all Armenians. Many songs were sung on free independent Armenia. The rich literature gives homage through poetry and prose rhyming on freedom and beauty. Mostly sad literature recollecting the sufferance of an enigmatic people always migrating and in exile, at the hope to see his homeland again, back to the land of his ancestors, back to its origin and integrity.

This explains my husband's attribution and disconcerted feeling towards suffering, poverty, and injustice. We were told that till the end of the 19th century there was an

Armenians community in Shanghai. Christian religion being tolerant, they had built a church, something that they are very good at. A few times we tried to locate the church but in vain.

Back to the Train

Now mother started to let some sort of complaints, not finding the purse in her bag. She was getting upset and sure than ever that she had not lost the purse. She emptied all her bag on the seat of the wagon, a gesture that left me very surprised and uneasy. Now I started to realise that mother did not find the purse in her bag. So I suggested very quietly and with a very small voice fearing what was unthinkable, to look in her other hand-bag. Of course my husband was not aware of this very quick and silent demonstration. Not willing to distract my husband's attention, unfortunately I couldn't succeed since the moment I brought down all the bags which belonged to my mother. At this my husband was very quick to ask why on earth was I bringing down all the suitcases, since we had some more time to reach to destination. I did not reply to my husband, but gave a side glance to mother. I started handling her suitcases and two other bags that she was carrying with. Now she was kneeling to open the bags one by one, and at each search her face was getting more flashed, deception and fear making her more and more uneasy. Even my children were quiet. My son were seeing his grandmother in that beaten and desolating position wanted to help her in her search. Therefore started pulling and pushing articles in her bag, each time with the hope of finding a small purse. But Hellas there was no sight of that historic purse. Now I started having doubts and thinking maybe I took back the purse in a hectic moment and that I had not realised my gesture and had put it in my bag. When you are very tired and under strong pressure the mind can play such obscene tours to memory which can sometimes leave big disappointment and a repercussion whose result might be devastating like in this case. I was so much convinced of my own thinking and picturing in my mind the gestures that in the end I was convinced definitely that the purse was with me!

I stood up this time to bring my hand-bag and started the same steps, looking up, seeking out, trying to track down. "Like mother like daughter," I emptied the articles of my bag this time on the floor.

Now I was encountering a very delicate issue, the fear of a forthcoming thunder was giving me disconcerting impulses and strong heart-beat. My husband had worked so hard to finalise all of our desires and was so happy and proud that we were accompanying him in his trip which was a prearranged business trip, eventually turned to a vacation trip.

Now my mind was playing and manifesting equivocal scenes based on desperate and urgent yearning of my heart to find a purse by miracle that my mind had already instigated like fancying for dunes in a mirage, lost in an arid and yellow desert having been tired and lost, thirsty and blazed under its incessant heat; thirsty hankering after the sacred source of water of deliverance and life.

My purse itself, the most banal of purses, does not worth much, but its plus-value was because of its content. It was carrying my jewels, worthing at least 250,000 to 300,000 thousand dollars and this is equal to a businessman's cost price. Panic was getting hold of me, I was starting to lose my temper and becoming out of countenance, no matter how hard I was trying to dispel the enfeeble thought. Sweat was covering my forehead till the root of my hair and out of fear I was not looking neither to my mother nor to my husband, since one had to tell me how come! The other to tell me, where is it?

Now my husband started getting intrigued, came closer to me and asked in a rather agitated voice: "Are you sure it was with you the time we left the hotel? You told me this morning when we met, you had kept the purse with your mother."

At this I looked at him and repeated the words in my mind to be sure that now this statement was the correct one, and I had to work on it, I turned to mother once again and asked: "Mother, are you sure you took the purse with you and you did not leave it in a hide place at the hotel?"

My mother looked worried and for the first time ever since our search, she looked inquisitive and worried. She was aware by this time that the purse was not in her handbags, neither mine. We had fetched thoroughly at every corner of our handbags; there remained only the big suitcases we had to wait to be in the hotel to be able to overhaul all the baggage to finally know what had happened to my expensive purse. Meanwhile in train they were announcing something in Chinese. Our attendant told us that we have to get ready, since we had reached the train station of the city of Canton (Guangzhou).

During and after our embarrassed search, we became suddenly very quiet. Everybody was looking for an answer to how and where this purse is. Thanks God my children with their innocent behaviour and positive attitude could cheer us and take us back to our predisposed reality. All the way my mind was enhancing me to calm down, providing new thoughts and new ways, to come out of my annoying situation.

Supposing that I would not find my purse, what would be the reaction of my husband? And that of my mother? Who was directly or indirectly implicated in this situation?! And then so what if I really, really lost it! It is not the end of the world. One has to be strong in front of such losses – it is only material loss, not the soul – would have added my sagacious grandma. But the point is that I was used to some of my jewellery pieces, and my husband would see the happening symbolically as a bad omen, not to mention the material loss which was not a small amount.

But there I start to have some anguish. I heard my husband talking to someone. Back to reality again, patient and resigned I waited for his accusations. Being pragmatic, he for sure wouldn't give up that quickly on the issue. Ensuing, he will tell me:

"You have been negligent, no comments!"

We reached our hotel, and my purse was forgotten for a while. The novelty of the place and the few expedients that we had to undertake before reaching the hotel made us forget all about it. We were hungry. My children were on their breakfast yet, having had some sandwiches in Hong Kong's train station. So the first thing we should do is to refresh ourselves. Being tired and hungry, we did not linger or spend time to change our dresses, and rushed to the dining room of the hotel which released the same smell as the main street of Hong Kong.

We were satiated and recovered the totality of our moods. My husband had to leave us for a few hours to talk with the people of his corporation. Mother was less talkative and more distracted every time I tried to bring her back from her daydream attitude. Unfortunately my mindfulness did not alter her self-denying position, absent and pensive unwilling to enjoy the moment.

My husband having left, I grasped the situation to ask her again: "Mother, are you sure you did not forget the purse at the hotel?

"You know Mom, it happens even to me, with my young age to forget my actions and deeds; everybody gets to that kind of stressful moments.

"I remember I gave it to you and you put it under the mattress, this is a hiding place

75

for your items ever since I remember from my childhood, so I am sure you left it there, you looked around but you forgot to look under the mattress, that's it, isn't it? Isn't it, mother? Please try to picture the last few hours before our departure."

This time the eyes of my mother started to open wide, as if suddenly she walked up from a nightmare, putting her both hands on her blushed face and remaining quiet for a while. There was again a big silence. This time my mother was talking with a calm voice weighing every word.

"Yes, I think you are right, absolutely right, that purse is lying under the mattress of my bed, and I totally forgot to take it out. Because the idea of our coming back was so convincing, and you know in the morning I was tired and upset with the children, well that's not the issue, but yes, the purse is well and nicely lying there, chance upon and come up with the hotel maids!"

I lay back on my chair; nothing could come out of my mouth. Suddenly I felt a strong fatigue, and urgent desire to sleep for a while. I asked the children to stay with grandma, and went up to our rooms, found a bed and lay down. I do not remember how many hours I have been sleeping there; when I opened my eyes the sun was setting down, a warm breeze was caressing my cheeks and I realised that I was still in my voyage outfits. Suddenly I felt sad and lonely and the first thought was for my mom. After our discussion I had let her alone with the children, she must have been exhausted and exasperated, bored with the children. I went down and I was thrilled at the sight of my children. They were now running towards me and each willing to hug me. My mother was sitting with my husband; they were relaxed but tense. I presumed my husband was informed of my purse's fate. When they saw me approaching to their table, they were both very happy and relieved, like you feel disconcerted after a long concert. I kissed both of them with sincere excuses for having been sleeping so many hours. My husband looked at me and said:

"I will have to call the hotel to see if they did find the purse 'under' the mattress." While he pronounced those words, he was pointing my mom. Of course me too. I was like sitting on a fire ready to take the defence of my mother. But fortunately my inter-vention was not necessary since my husband left the table to go and try to call the hotel.

I sat there with my mom annoyed and astonished at the turning of the events. My mother and I were having the same thought! How if the maid took the purse and not declare to the hotel? Who would not be tempted of that treasure with cash dollars and exquisite jewels!

Effectively, once again our hopes to recuperate the purse sank, like the Titanic, sinking at the ebb of the waters.

"What Goes Around Comes Around"

How could I expect that my purse could be recoverable? Who on earth would give back such a big amount to his owner! It is a matter of luck. To strengthen my belief and recover some of my hope, I was almost loosing ground with my personal strength and belief going through acute analysis with logical consequential steps of the situation at hand. Unfortunately, facing the controversial incident, for the first time in my life, I was having doubts on the human character. I was discriminating the human strength towards greed and desire to material and covetous to acquired richness.

Suddenly I was brought back from my deep silence to surface my tangible and objective reality. My husband was there watching me and shaking his head maliciously. Of course at first instance I could not realise the outcome of his gesture, but then I realised that it had to do with the fatal telephone to Hong Kong. I waited for him to go on. He had a way to beat about the bush. Initially at that fated moment, that character of his seemed so erroneous. Time had stopped, I was seeing only the face of my herald and like a sick man's desperate hope, I was waiting for the sentence of expectation and faith, which makes our world go round. Yes he went on, chewing every word, "You are both lucky, because the purse is found and untracked in the hands of my friend Mr. Chen (the hotel owner). You are lucky because you met the most honourable and exquisite person in my whole existence." I could not wait to hear the other precious words pouring from my husband's sincere and honest soul towards another good and wonderful person, Mr. Shu, my old wonderful Chinese friend. I jumped from my chair and looked around my mother, who having heard the good news started to sob. Not having the force to stand up, I went to her. I kneeled in front of her skinny and beautiful knees and took her hands in mine to say:

"Mother, it is over, this time we were lucky, really and truly lucky. Lucky to have encountered a man, a Chinese man of a generation, who I hope, is not fading or dying away. A man that owned the world in his heart, who was one with universe and God!"

The Reminiscence of My Chinese Old Friend

Later on when I was handed over my purse, nothing was missing, nothing. Everything was there, sparkling and attractive, beautiful and tempting to appeal and attract even a king. Maybe our benefactor Mr. Shu was tempted too. This feeling is something that I will never know of course.

I shook his hand vigorously, since I could not hug or kiss him. It was not in the old Chinese traditional rules of conduct. Therefore respecting that reality not to upset him to shake his old and tired hands, wrinkled prematurely out of hardship and not taking care of his skin.

Initially my mother and I had a profound respect towards him, even before this unprecedented event. He had been working in that hotel ever since he had arrived to Hong Kong and he was in charge of our room that he did it with a special care and interest. We treated him with respect in regard to his age, like a grandfather and not like a personel of the hotel.

My mother was considerate and respectful, offering small presents to his children or grand children, which of course was a very difficult act to undertake, knowing his dignified attitude towards presents and pourboire. But with time he realised our intentions were that of sincere friendship, and a gesture of gratitude that we were showing towards his heed and extra kindness. He used to pamper us with special care, arranging the room and fulfilling all our desires, to make us feel at home. If we happen to have another personel in charge for that particular day, he would come personally to attend the cleaning, or if he was absent, he would ask if everything was done according to our desire.

After we recovered from our emotions, he told us how he found the purse. He went on saying thereafter we left the place; he had to prepare the rooms for another family. So he was asked by the supervising manger to make up the rooms that we had occupied for such long time. Subsequently he went on saying, "That was something good, considering the fact and presuming that you might have forgotten a few things; and my fears were well established. Honestly nothing was left behind, unless the one you had decided, alluding to the suitcases we handled beforehand.

"The moment I wanted to change the bed-sheet, my fingers touched something hard under the mattress. To my big amazement reaching my hand underneath, I found this purse of yours," showing by his tiny fingers. "First I thought it belonged to the children, and only after I opened it that I realised the big mistake you had made. Luckily I managed to clean up the room!"

We all started to laugh, a laughter of happiness of joy and gratitude for having found a virtuous man, a man of honour, a rich man, whose heart was so big to carry so much compassion and generosity. For us he was the richest man in Hong Kong, whose reminiscence I still cherish. My children were too young, unfortunately, to have memory of the events, unless the story that we kept on telling and praising the worthy Chinese riche in virtue and honour. Chinese people had a very old and strong philosophical background, that was in a way their religious upbringing and social righteous behaviour. They always praised virtue and dignity and conscious behaviour, straightforwardness, the endowment of giving and sharing.

Despite our shifted moods, we found some consolation in the new and the unknown. I cannot confirm today undeniably, if on that particular trip I saw much of China, but it was the beginning of a prevalent experience. We entered from a narrow door like all foreigners, but the most important issue and realisation was that the door was gliding and letting big open through the years, to reveal its present, which was getting better and more impelling. The ruins much neglected were starting to become centres of interest. Reminiscence of the past glorious history was pushing them forward to the conquest of the present. The sagacity is the lessons they acquired in their past history, and their present is their faith in strong and prosperous nation for a future which will disclose itself through intransigent and dedicated conveyance.

Between this trip and the ones I undertook with my husband during two decades were undertaking and committed ventures of discovery!

> The more ancient a nation is, the more her titles of glory are authentic; and the more we see her concern about the past of her language.
>
> Omar Färrükh (a Lebanese author), *Autocritics*

Guangzhou

I undertook my second trip to Guangzhou (Canton) alone with my husband. I must say I felt a little nostalgic not having my beautiful group with me.

While in the train I was recalling their presence and picturing and coveting their childish inquisitive behaviour, nosy-puckering and snoopy questions, followed by their laughter. While seeping my tea their dislike towards the yellow-brown drink made me laugh each time the service attendant would bring the cha to our compartment, something that they could not yet appreciate. Of course the event which had inappropriately occurred had shaken up my mother, who, when hearing that I was going to Canton again, had a big smile and said:

"Do not forget to salute my Chinese friend Mr. Shu in Hong Kong, the most virtuous and honourable man I ever met in my whole existence!"

The most interesting thing that I recall from my Canton trip is my invitation to the restaurant by the corporation. In those days that was a privilege considering all the foreigners that were visiting the country, not everybody had that kind of treat. I was very happy at last to be alone with real Chinese people. Needless to say that the whole day I was walking and visiting the "Fair." That time it was the most important fair in China. Many foreigners would come from abroad to attend and purchase. I was struck with the prices so attractive and workable to our different markets, all kinds of commodities, hand crafts were fabulous regarding table cloths, to bed-covers, china and porcelain sets. I was taken by their abundance and lucrative business. The eagerness and the concern of the corporations to collaborate and endeavour to the success of the business was omnipotent. Of course those were the 1970s yet. Although China wanted to enter the world market so they needed competent businessmen from all over the world, things were not that easy as they seemed. China was starting to caveat the situation in order to bring forth strong dollars. He was aiming more to export for that issue, and he could jungle with the very low prices ensuing the fact that Chinese people did not earn much. The competition was very severe for the outside world, who still dazzled not taking into serious consideration the out-coming policy of Mainland China. Notwithstanding for us the main issue was our business. The problems that we encountered in our business were due to ever-going changes in the government whose repercussion was felt within the corporations. Therefore the people with whom we were supposed to make the deals were always changing and therefore we were obliged each time to commit ourselves giving credentials, and intrinsic explanations about the business in general, which was time and energy consuming. There were no written statements where each encounter or business transaction was registered. There was no basic structure of how and why the business was registered. Their only concern in those days was the effected transaction, the interest, and the fulfillment of the contract. Our relation was based on friendship and co-operation. We let politicians fight for their differences. Businessmen are apolitical on surface; all they care about is their business. But when the amount swells to be very attractive and lucrative, every-body has an eye on it. Another behaviour was very peculiar with Chinese corporation dealing with customers. They had a predilection and preference to work with new castomers. It was a wise, subtce and shread step towards business and a traditional attitude in general.

The reminiscence of my visits on the other hand was mostly attributed and was marked with their subtle long friendship enhanced with special treatment.

I never went walking in the streets alone, for being a foreigner, I was a centre of attraction. Nothing was premeditated during such tours in the city, a sudden crowd would be formed to approach my person, to inspect and get a closer look to my physical features; not to forget my outfit, which was so much in contrast with their own outfits.

Another important reality was the language barrier. Not many people spoke English, or any other foreign language, except the government personnel. Today most of the Chinese learn foreign languages and they speak fluently, what a tremendous assiduous change, to challenge an undertaking, a momentum, to achieve a big vicissitude, to bolster and boost their new lives, to convey an extensive change in their status, to bring about a hale and hearty society, a backbone for the future offspring.

My Predilection on Women Issue

We were rather a large group of men and only one lady, an issue that annoyed me personally as a woman among men. In the working hours there were always several women working around in the offices of the corporation: typing, calculating, or serving cha, and then suddenly during invitations or banquets, they would become less in number or almost out of traffic! Well, it was only after that particular invitation that I took conscious of this issue, where tradition was enforced with the socialist ideology of that time. Again it is an sensitive issue of East and West social preferences that I was apprehending slowly year after year. Candidly I thought that was the way the corporation rationalised, but effectively the averment lies in the behaviour of the Chinese lady vis-à-vis its society. Very protective and reserved, ensuing an inhibition to personal concept, but a traditional social and moral ethic for them. Dealing with matters of having fun, drinking and relaxing, women was denied the entrance to the big door, a favourable pretext "the tradition." Thanks God, today in the beginning of the 21st century, things are changing for women in China.

Unfortunately many revolutions could straighten up China's status as a big nation but could not altogether revolutionise and straighten up old and stagnated behaviour and many-century-old ideologies. This issue needs to be reconsidered and roles need to be redefined on relation and equality of men and women. The constraint attitude is as old as mankind, unfortunately so much incarcerated and profoundly rooted that it needs a bigger effort to bring forth a more equitable and just place for women in China. They brought forth their contribution in the changes that China undertook for centuries long, especially in the 20th century. They fought hard side by side with men.

One day I met a Chinese woman wearing so simple and looking so beautiful and natural. She was wearing a very plain suit sparkling clean, with pants so wide that her two legs could get in very easily. If it were in our countries, I would say it is the fashion, well with her that was not the issue, but anyhow, she was rather a nice-looking and pleasant lady, she spoke good English, which facilitated our sitting, therefore her presence became a must, considering the fact that not all members of the delegation spoke English. But not once I met that lady to any of our banquets, suddenly she was not indispensable!

They needed to hear our assessment to conclude their smart conclusion, scrutinising our behaviour, firmness of character or deep thoughts. We watched, analysed, and observed. Every issue or assessment was translated, alluding to incentive motivation, lure, and suggestion. We were constantly questioned, attentively heard, appreciated, and applauded. Every time something important was declared to the benefit of the corporation as an impetus and enticement. With time I started to get used to that demeanour too, therefore I started to appreciate and clapped my hands just like them, to accompany the chorus of cheerfulness. It was so much fun to be with them, this other side of the world, sitting and sharing happy moments, with people who objectively had no relation with us besides business transaction!

There Was a Snake on My Table

In Europe, restaurants are either on the first floor, or on the highest level of a building, say tenth floor and up, with the basic idea to take a glimpse of the city's view. But this special restaurant did not follow this norm; while reaching there many street people were hailing us at the corner of the street. To my big surprise, the restaurant was on the fourth floor of the building.

We were in the middle of a very clean, all white floor, sparkling immaculate, with round tables, covered with white starched-iron table-clothes, with napkins so white that it makes you think they were small neon lights fixed and arranged in the shape of swans. The centre piece had an elevated round pivot table-centre which I found so clever and practical; it took me ten years to have one of those on my table, reminding me from time to time of that very first special tête-à-tête with the corporation.

Behind us was the very Chinese screens of black lacer, with the design of dragon, which was watching me with his fiery eyes so audaciously, to make sure that I was not of the group. This richly dressed lady in scarlet colour gave him a nostalgic emotion of his past prosperous days, where Chinese ladies were wrapped in silken gowns hand-embroidered overalls, with the most exquisite designs, bearing his embroidered picture of "dragon" on their chests despite men preferred to carry it embroidered on the back of their gowns, to be energized through its powerful token.

I looked around again, well, that was the only symbol of the glorious past of China. Each of us had one waiter serving and attending us on the table. We had all kinds of drinks starting with Moutai (a Chinese wine) which is very strong. I had to drink in the name of all our emancipated women and I did it. My husband was a little worried knowing that I was not used to drink that sort of strong drinks.

The dulcet dishes were following one after the other. We had starters such as the eggs of different animals, such as very small pigeon eggs, prepared in a very special way, then thread like salty things of different colours – green, yellow and red, dried and died. And they were the eggs of a certain animal, but frankly I do not recall of which animal. Then came the very famous stew, what a gustatory momentum, which makes part of any Chinese dinner. It was very tasty, with creamy colour. There were white pieces of meat floating in it like the wings of the chicken, without the skin. First I thought it was so, but our friend Mrs. Chang had a very hearty laughter seeing my reflection and tried to press on me like a game of guessing to palate out the bites that I was starting to swallow and judge the origin of the animal. This restaurant is a very famous one renown for its exotic exquisite cuisine. Then I saw my husband having a malicious smile so as to tell me – "Hem, my wife, you are in a very special land with amazing customs, a rich land where you can expect anything, and everything. They are the origin of many civilisations, many strange and amazing things have taken root in this country." Now Mr. Hu went on saying: "You are eating the flesh of a snake, a very big snake." All this was said with calm and certain pride.

Meanwhile coming down on like a bolt from the blue, I must have blushed so much out of my shock that I was quickly offered a cup of water, even though my gestures were constrained. I was behaving in an exemplary ethic, like a big girl. Suddenly we got all very silent. I tried to smile a gesture of recapitulation, and reconciliation. But again Mr. Hu came to my rescue. "Mrs. Alex, the meat of snake is very exclusive (a polite word not to say expensive) and very healthy. In old times they used to give to pregnant women (of course only rich women could afford, he wanted to imply) to have healthy children." I started to laugh since the idea of being pregnant again made me laugh, because for me that was done, I already have had three children till the age of twenty-five, so no, thank you. But I might need a healthy body which is even, if not, more important to go on living with health and beauty towards a promising future. I raised my spoon inclined in front of so much solicitation to satiate and comply to eat the soup which was starting to get cold. This time with predilection and knowledge in full consciousness and gustatory appreciation, what I was sending to my organism was pieces of food to acquire health and everlasting beauty. Yes I went on this time convincing myself, I had to eat, a gusto based on the curiosity and the new to enhance my palate. It really had the taste of chicken, very mild taste, easy to eat. The idea disturbing me was that I was eating a snake. Notwithstanding the inquisitive faces of our hosts, I dived my spoon again in the soup and started with appropriation to swallow my stew. We were offered a second round of the course, and to prove again my allotment, I did not refuse the serving. Despite all this, I was starting to recover my speech and giving my appreciation on the taste, trying to swallow my bewildered mood thus animating my hosts who felt so happy and satisfied with this ignorant foreigner who was going to ruin their invitation.

Now that the dishes were emptied, like the unseen hand of Epicure (the god of food and merriment), I had a new dish in front of me, ravishing and disdainful on the white tablecloth. And I was not finished with the surprises of this astonishing and weird invitation full of contriving attempts. This was becoming a battlefield of food, to dine and wine. What a paradox, some people would be thrilled, like my husband – to be on this table, at my place. The second round began. I glanced at my dish, this time the china was of another design, rather brick and black with some yellow, to give a stronger aspect to the food in the dish. It was a sort of plane pieces of chicken or fish I could not say for sure, accompanied with some stewed and steamed vegetables, a cooking style that I learned later in China and became an expert.

This time, out of curiosity, I started to dive in the food. I had become fearless and summon to contest, thinking that after you ate a snake nothing could be more impugn! What could be more exotic, alien, and untried to make me ill at ease and out of place! After my first bite of that unknown piece of meat I saw again the eyes of my hosts and that of my husband focusing on me. Now I was looking more merry due to all the wine I was sipping which made its effect on me, thus my cheeks were burning red and my eyes shining out of excitement. If they would ask me to sing or dance, I would have executed since my emotions high up and swinging in the enchantment, in this friendly and welcoming exotic atmosphere. But instead they were telling me to eat, so I was eating, and guess what the most exclusive food in Guangzhou or maybe in all China in those days was. How could I refuse this much cordial and generous invitation! Truly these people were showing a high respect and wanted to tighten their relation with us because they needed our collaboration. It was a synergy, a situation, where we needed each other's contribution. They were in need of new ways or know-how, and we were in need of artful hands reliable, dynamic, and fulfilling to enhance a flourishing business through competitive and lucrative prices.

Now I was enjoying my food, meanwhile asking what I was chewing since I was told that it was a special animal too.

"Mrs. Han, what are we eating?" I asked the lady. Mrs. Han turned and said, "It is a very exclusive animal, and we can eat only on special occasions." Oh yes! That much I could rather understand, but what I wanted to know was: what kind of exclusivity is it, does it have fur? I went on questioning. This time our chief host interfered adding, "Yes." Then there was a silence. "Well," I went on asking again, "is it a monkey?" There was a chorus of laughter, and then a flat "No." Again I was silent. I was trying to solve the puzzle! It has fur; it lives in the jungle; it is not a monkey. Prior to my visit to China, I was told by my husband that he had eaten monkey brain in a very exclusive ceremony in Hong Kong, therefore jumping to conclusion assuming maybe after the snake, I was going to try the monkey, if not the brain but the other parts of the monkey! I was reaching almost to the last bite of my food; we could see the beautiful face of an exotic cat at the bottom of my dish. I started to admire the motif, and the refine drawing, the head of a beautiful cat smiling at my face. Then again I started to give a thought assuming to solve this unequalled and unprecedented situation in my culinary experiences, although after so many fork-bites, the solution was not in my mouth. While I was still dining, my eyes fell upon the drawing of my adjoining guest who turned and said, "Do you like cats?" I said, "Yes, of course. Ever since my childhood I recall having domestic animals at home, cats, dogs, birds, especially the 'love birds', turtles and rabbits." And I went on telling the story of my young sisters and their aversion to taste cooked rabbit meat, ever since my father though with a big regret had to kill their beautiful rabbits in a sort their friends, as an urgent step to stop their incredible propagation. In an apartment it is difficult to raise so many domestic animals even if that apartment was 500 meters square.

There was a big silence again. I refused to refill my cup with wine, since I was beginning to feel its dazzling effects on my neurones of getting me talkative; at least that's how I felt. I was not getting talkative but rather I was jumping to conclusion because then my assumptions that "the end will justify the means" or the truth about me eating a wild cat will justify their silence and their fear of a deception. But here I had to pertain a cool and reserved position not to give another shock to these coherent cheerful groups, who were getting on the road to appreciate our friendly and condescend attitude. I think from that day on I knew how to win the heart of my Chinese encounters, how to make them understand my feelings and ideas when their English was not that polished and my Chinese resumed to two words: *Xiexie ni* (thank you) or *hen hao* (good, nice) or *bu hao* (bad). In one word, we were able to communicate with the language of the heart and reasoning. I was eating a cat. I went on saying, but a wild one that saved little bit my bad consciousness. It is an exotic cat, a big one, as I was explained, very rare, living in the mountainous area north of China.

I was stunned that being a wild cat, it had very soft meat and rather tasty. Notwithstanding it was tastier than the serpent. Cats are our domestic tiny-whiny little creatures that we cuddle and cherish even though they do not carry gratifying attitude towards their adoptive parents. Cats are spiritual animals you cannot tame, so you should have a very special attitude to read and understand their behaviour. Dogs on the other hand are more friendly and faithful which gives them the trophy as man's best friend.

The reminiscence of that culinary art was of an unequalled experience of presentation and demonstration of taste and design comely and surprisingly unequalled. And so much work time and care was for decorating and flourishing. There was so much to learn and appreciate. The dessert of fruits was followed by ice-cream.

Well, honestly, that was just the beginning of my culinary adventure and the discovery by getting acquainted to the exotic dishes that I had to encounter on my trips in different provinces from east to west and south to north with their different taste and preparation, and mostly different ingredients.

Today I cook most renowned and easily provided and prepared Chinese food of different provinces, prepared with the most common ingredients to handle. On different occasions or in other provinces, I experienced amazing and exotic food of different taste and ingredients that I had to eat with a smile on my face and gratitude in my heart.

We got out of the restaurant. The weather was a little bit cooler, effectively cooling down my mood with all the food and wine I ingested in the restaurant.

Suddenly one tall Chinese from our group came closer to me, a person with whom I did not have the chance to exchange many words.

"Mrs. Alex, did you notice this window there?" He pointed to me a huge glass window near the main entrance door, a wide aquarium like window that in reality was the dwelling of big snakes of three to four meters in length, of different colours, thick and wide like a baby elephant's leg. There were so many of them, sliding up and down on the wooden logs, especially designed for their purpose. I looked at them for a long time, of course the others had followed us, then the same tall gentleman who had kept quiet all during dinner courses had become suddenly very communicative and eager to add his part of the speech and finalise the evening by saying, "Mrs. Alex, the snake you ate are similar to those displayed here. They are very special and rare species." This sight could not leave my husband indifferent. He approached me, not to say jumped; himself was taken by surprise. He was flabbergasted, perplex, looking at me and added, "You know, even I didn't know they were snakes of that size."

We have told this story many times in our encounters a decade back. People would be amazed at our recollection and adventure. Today people are more aware of the different tastes and palate to encounter in the world. It is like a big garden, people willing to enjoy the exotic and the different with leisure and curiosity. Openness is the right tag. Curiosity and acceptance bring ideas, cultures, and ideologies under a new spot light. This is why food talks about the history and culture of a country.

The language of food is the heart and undertaking of nations. Today at the threshold of the twenty-first century, margins got narrower; acceptance about the other's food becomes more lenient and appreciating. Chinese in the last decade or so started to eat hamburger, pizza, drink milk and try to eat cheese or other dairy products. After the Second World War, they started to eat beef, something that was not very common.

The topic of food is a large one, its language conveyed on every aspect and translation. When you are served on a prerequisite and welcoming table, happy to share their bread, that is an important moment to draw feelings and emotions high. My husband and I had so many such cherished moments with corporations and friends. Those were the times when they were not yet living in the plenty but they wanted to show their hospitality and allotment to their foreign counterparts. I enjoyed each and every one of them, the different provinces and cities that I visited, each having one thing in common, their sense of friendship, hankering to success, struggling to reach to a better result and mostly their hospitality through dinners and banquets, honouring the guest and making him feel important.

There are differences between me and the foreigner – who either lived there all year long, or was born and raised there, since in my case I was the visitor, who dealt with money, business, with hard currency. I dealt mainly with the staff of the different corporations that were designated to fulfil and covet their obligations towards the company although that relation did not facilitate our status of business people, guest of the company, there were always clean cut barriers. We were always the last to know when there was a change in the corporation, they never showed their feelings, already it is a custom, and with the different instructions and the fear of the foreigner made them more reserved and cautious. I had the feeling that there was always a curtain between them and me, something that bothers me even today. Of course I knew and respected their cautious attitude, but again I loved transparency. I did make friends no matter what. I could win their hearts and their confidence and through honesty and transparency. Some of them visited us in Switzerland, they studied our behaviour in respect to our proper environment, therefore they found that we were not different, our demeanours and functioning were the same, as when we were in their country. We were somehow similar, sharing and hankering the same dreams but on different scales.

Le roi est mort, vive le roi neuf (The King Passed Away, Long Live the New King)

This is how history of all nations is forged. We read about big leaders, eminent kings, and emperors who have changed the course of history. Some figures impressed me while I was discovering their legacy and bestowal thus patrimonies. They are people that the world has acknowledged, therefore they deserve the respect and owe of the future generations. The list being long, I chose personalities who mostly deal with the subject of my book, and my predilection.

Tutankhamun, the young pharaoh of Egypt. Alexander the Great of Macedonia. Mohammed, the prophet of all Arabs. Saladin Ayoubi, the Arab king. Elizabeth I of Britain. Napoleon Bonaparte, the French Emperor. Peter the Great of Russia. Abraham Lincoln of USA. Lenin, Stalin and Migoyan of the former Soviet Union. Gandhi of India. Che Guevara. Martin Luther King. Yitzhak Rabin of Israel. Mandella of South Africa.

China is a big nation due to the fact that there were always big shakers and movers. During the names I admire, there are: Empress Wu Zetian, the only female monarch in Chinese history; Genghis Khan, the creator of the largest empire of the world; Lin Zexu, China's fighting spirit against the United Kingdom and all other Western invaders; Mao Zedong (Mao Tsetung), one of the biggest leaders of the 20th century; Zhou Enlai, the most popular leader in China from 1949 to 1976; last but not least, Deng Xiaoping, the most influential figure in Chinese history of the 20th century.

In my frequent trips, I saw China's face changing in its politically social and economical climate. Personally I have a tremendous respect towards China's culture and philosophy, history and people witnessing a new history. Deep down I know that a big country is always big, you can not judge a nation by some eras, since countries are like the season of the nature, having their cycles and periods when they are more productive and fruitful than other cycles dormant and arid. On each of my trips to China, I saw some major changes, either in their business organization or openness towards the outside world, yet very cautious and with great tactic, very choosy and subtle not to rush on the inutile. It was a give-and-take policy, but the giver, in this case China, was never interested to buy and accommodate what he is not willing to consume. Luxury items were still a distant reality till the beginning of the 1990s, as well as jewelry was only an item for export and rarely to be used by the natives themselves. Of course today things have changed tremendously and this is why I love China.

The best rulers are those whose existence is merely known by the people.
The next best are those who are loved and praised.
The next are those who are feared.
And the next are those who are despised.
It is only when one does not have enough faith in others that others will have no faith in him.
The great rulers value their words highly.
They accomplish their task; they complete their work.
Nevertheless, their people say that they simply follow nature.

Lao Tzu, *Tao-Te-Ching*

Nanjing, Jiangsu

Back to Nanjing

As we were leading our pearl business in Switzerland, my husband had to go very often to China to bring forth rough material (pearls), for the sake of our small industry, to select, categorize, treat and string. Pearls were for making suitable bunches to be redistributed to customers all over the world, especially to the Middle Eastern countries, which were the biggest customers for these categories of pearls. Of course for the Chinese economy, this business was not that important, having in mind all the huge industries and joint ventures at hand. But nonetheless it was important for us, and for our corporations, who were undertaking a huge task to bring forth a flourishing business.

I did some of these trips accompany my husband and a few times we did the schedule with the whole family.

We were now in the 1980s, China was starting to become more lenient, encouraging foreign investors, thus many hotels of every size and renown names were being constructed in the main cities like Shanghai, Beijing, Nanjing (Nanking), and so on. We were lucky that we stayed in one of these motels on the outskirts of Nanjing. The motel was built by an Australian, which is a brand-new building. We were among the first customers, along with some American tourists of third age, who were so surprised to find a whole family – young couples with their three children – coming from Europe, expressed by them "the old continent," soaring from the top of Mount Zermatt (mostly that was pronounced by the group), landed at the heart of China. They were clapping their hands excitedly and happily as if we were lost and found in the middle of that "antique continent", the old capital of historic China, Nanjing. They were a charming group, most of whom coming from the state of Washington, all pensioned men and women, who were there to enjoy a vacation, and thus to have a direct contact with the people of China. They were very charming and full of knowledge. They praised the city of Nanjing, but complained for not being introduced to the temples and historical sites of the city and its surroundings. They had a defined program and they had to execute and follow accordingly.

Their second complaint was that they could not eat American hamburgers, something that was not conceivable in those days. Hong Kong was enjoying that privilege and many other privileges long time ago. Americanization and its influence started in the 1990s. Coca cola was the first to make its gentle intrusion, next was huge investors with their million-dollar investing in huge plants, hotels and joint ventures, followed by McDonald's, Pizza Hut, and others.

Unfortunately we could not acquaint more with the tourists, since they had to keep on with their tight tour program of southeast China. I was a little bit disappointed, but it only lasted a few hours, since our tight program of the following days took away all my other worries to concentrate on the new and surprising.

It was one of those days when the sun was high up in the sky. We had been to one of the sights of the pearl premises so the delegation had decided to have a walk at the heart of the city.

Eminent Capital

After we parted our overwhelmed crowd, we returned to our hotel, merry and enchanted having acquainted with the citizens of Nanjing, the royal antique city of China, rich in history and political importance of about 5,000 years. Nanjing is the capital of Jiangsu Province. It had also its economic importance along its region, becoming a centre of weaving, especially brocade and metal foundries. The modern city, when first I discovered, was not so comely. It was old and dusty, with some high buildings, but it had a beautiful natural surrounding of gardens, parks, lakes, and of course the Yangtze River. Its rich history as the capital of so many dynasties made me so much attracted to it, considering its antique heritage of pagodas, pavilions and towers. A patrimony to show the importance of Nanjing who has played an important role in the Chinese history undeniably, beyond any question. It had become the capital of so many short-lived dynasties especially the Southern Dynasties during the 5th - 6th centuries. It had been the southern capital during the Ming Dynasty (14th - 17th centuries) by Emperor Zhu Yuanzhang. In 1911, with the overthrow of Manchus and the establishment of the Republic, Nanjing became the seat of the Nationalist government of Kuomintang in the 20th century. This explains the presence of the Mausoleum of Doctor Sun Yat-Sen who is considered the father of modern China. Nanjing today embraces an amazingly high technological development. It has become an important industrial base for automobiles, electronics, and machine tool industries, petrochemicals production, steel foundries and in aeronautics.

The Yangtze and Its Counterparts and Parallels

Besides contributing to the natural beauty, Yangtze River offered strategic protection and made an important gateway for trade and shipping.

One beautiful morning, our corporation invited us to have a boat tour on the Yangtze River. We drove very early that morning, since in July, the weather was rather humid and hot, at noon it used to reach its climax where you might think you are breathing not air but rather steam, mixed with moist and the putrid smell of the nearby houses, elongated with their narrow and dusty pavements. It would not be exaggerating when I say Nanjing is one of the hottest cities in China during summer.

There were almost no cars early that morning, only some big factory cars and three-wheeled bikes. We walked along a very impressive bridge and a totally new picture was being drawn in front of me, a masterwork of a modern advanced architecture at the heart of Nanjing. This is China, exactly this reality took me by surprise. You could not predict, never understand. You could not measure its potential or conclude its capacity. At that moment I knew that nothing would stop the advance of China, its determination was as hard as those steels. Its will was like those stones unchanging and steadfast in its nature, yet drawn to be faceted with intelligence and subtlety. A wide bridge was made of steel and stone, double decked (the second deck was for railways) of 6,500 meters long. Our guide was explaining with pride that the bridge was built in China.

He went on explaining that it had been started by the Russians, who left China at the beginning of the 1960s, and took all the plans with them. And our guide added proudly – that the bridge was completed by Chinese afterwards. The year I was cross-passing the bridge, it was only a decade old.

I do not exaggerate if I say that Yangtze is a very famous river of China, like many counterpart rivers in different parts of the world. An affinity and facsimile example is the "Danube" which is a river passing many major cities in Europe, especially Austria. A legendary river that has inspired big musicians like Johann Strauss, who composed the very famous and exquisite waltz *The Blue Danube.*" Another river is another example, the river Moldau crossing and irrigating East Europe. A homage of un-equalled treasure was rendered to the river by the Finnish composer Sibelius, who composed the "Moldau," a beautiful symphony so much appreciated for its soft and vibrating melody that thrills all your emotions, making you feel the movements of the river through the subtle language of the music. This is the itinerary of a river drawn on the unseen rope of notes, so vibrant, so harmoniously, and rhythmically arranged.

The Russian Volga was an inspiration for so many writers. So many songs have been sung, alluring to its enticing beauty. So many poets have written poems of sorrow and sadness, songs of lovers having parted, or abandoned mother's tears of on its reefs, wailing the departure of their beloved children for the so-called vindicated wars.

Euphrates River has its fountainhead in Armenia (a small land in the Caucasus, on the border line with the former Soviet Union). The important mass of the river

A wind, bringing willow-cotton, sweetens the shop,
And a girl from Wu, pouring wine, urges me to share it.
With my comrades of the city who are here to see me off,
And as each of them drains his cup, I say to him in parting,
Oh, go and ask this river running to the east
If it can travel farther than a friend's love!
                    Li Po, "Parting at a Wine-shop in Nanking"

irrigates the neighbouring Arabic peninsula crossing mainly Iraq, the old Babylonian country of 5,000 years old. Euphrates is a very famous river for many decades, having and playing an important role in the history of the region. Many significant battles have been lost and won around it. Many nomads, merchants, soldiers, kings and prophets (the Christening of John the Baptist, the New Testament) have swum in its depth. This is why its name was recited and mentioned in literature for centuries, especially from the days when Arabs were and are still dominating those regions.

Besides being the longest river in the world, the Nile is as old as mankind civilisation, tracing back some seventy centuries of history, from the Pharaohs to its eminent role in the prophecy of the *Bible* – the story of Baby Moise, the "great prophet," was found in the waters of the Nile by the daughter of the Pharaoh (Old Testament in the *Bible*) – and in the Jewish Tora. Napoleon, the French Emperor, fought near its waters in 1798, in the area of the Nile Delta. Napoleon's expedition gave rise to "Egyptology" which became its true victory. In another word, the heritage of cultural enlightenment ensued. The scholars that accompanied Napoleon Bonaparte's scientific expedition to Egypt included mathematicians, astronomers, engineers, and architects, who under very arduous and difficult situations overcame dangers, deciphered the Nile banks treasure, which became the world's richest museum. They excavated the monolithic obelisks to the vast statues, tombs, and temples covered with mystical drawings and hieroglyphs (holy writings in Greek language). They also tried to uncover the secrets of the Egyptian civilisation and mostly studied the influence of the Nile on the fertility of the country, on the irrigation system, on agriculture arts and crafts. Some years later, on the edge of the Nile Delta, the big discovery of the *Rosetta stone* ensued. It was a stone of one meter square and 762 kilo in weight, where the same text was engraved in three different languages: in hieroglyphics at the top, Arabic in the middle, and Greek at the bottom. Jean François Champollion was the man who finally deciphered the mystery of the hieroglyphs, which opened the way to Egyptology, an inventory of the history and mystery of the Pharaoh. Egyptian adventure triggered all kinds of excavation such as the Tomb of Tutankhamun, which was discovered by Howard Carter. All these aroused a big interest towards the Egyptian Pharaonic culture. Many politicians, financiers, and merchants poured from around the world on the banks of the Nile, all in search of bargains, sometimes pillaging the ancient remains of the cultural inventory.

Thus the Nile, besides being the rich cultural cradle of the Pharaonic civilisation, is the cradle of several other civilisations, such as the famous Mameluke. It also irrigates most of the lands of Egypt.

The impelling and interesting archaeological discoveries and tombs reminds me of the Qin Terracotta of China in Shaanxi Province. The Terracotta warriors and horses are magnificent discovery as early as 1974 nearby the tomb of Qin Shi Huang who became the first emperor of China. He ascended to the throne at the age of thirteen (in 246 BC). The Emperor Qin, just like the Pharaohs in Egypt, prepared his mausoleum which took eleven years to finish, and just like the Pharaohs, he took all his treasures and sacrificial objects and buried them with him for the big voyage after death, the same obsession and the same belief!

The sight was uncovered accidentally by peasants digging well near the royal tomb in the city of Xi'an. There is a big museum now which features this life size terracotta figures of warriors and horses, altogether seven thousand pottery soldiers, horses chariots, and weapons which have been unearthed from several pits. The famous archaeological sight was opened to the public for the first time in 1979. My husband and I were among the privileged to see those newly discovered columns of man-size earthen soldiers, followed by wooden war chariots at the back of the soldiers. It is a world patrimony and heritage listed by UNESCO in the year 1987.

Journeying to the new continent, crossing through the north then to the southern states in USA, we come across the Mississippi-Missouri, the longest river in the world, of about 6,260 km. From the region of the great lakes in the north to the Gulf of Mexico to the south trespassing Saint Louis, Memphis, and mainly the New Orleans, henceforth it was also the blessed reefs, the home of freshwater shells, henceforth a treasured river, the ebb for the natural pearls, especially the long, big pearls. The Mississippi was first discovered by the Spanish in the 16th century, later on, only in the 17th century, explored by Marquette, Joliet and Cavalier de La Salle. Since then it is a very important fluvial way. Being very important and contributing to the welfare of the surrounding cities, many folksongs have been attributed as a homage to the river.

Tracking many such rivers in the world that have inspired and enchanted poets and composers to write and sing their importance and their contemporary merit through the centuries.

Artists all over China were inspired by Yangtze's beauty, its trail and its contribution in history. There are many landscapes painted by famous painters. We can find in history and literary books poems and songs of praise written on its behalf, expounding the spirit and the grandeur and propounding the static beauties of the lands, meanwhile building up history's important plights and fights of warriors, the story of banished lovers, of fortune seekers, and the widow wailing to seek her husband's return.

So you can understand my enthusiasm and excitement when we got in an old motor boat of small cruises, which had to take us to the track of the river with its different sights and fertile spots. So much green I had not seen since I left Switzerland, actually not this type of chlorophyll, and such diversified trees and bushes, some of them very special to me. For the first time I made a close relation with the Chinese scrolls and paintings depicting scenery of trees and hillsides. The landscape which was initiating before our very eyes made a relation to the paintings of landscapes on parchment and porcelains. I concluded that those works of arts were not the imagination of artists but the copy of their living inspiration towards their surrounding nature. Well there I was engulfed, trapped in my own enthusiasm. The picture was precise, enthralled and wondering, with legitimate signatures, yet so ephemeral since there were no magical hands to freeze those moments. The instant picture was a matter of technicality through the cold touch of the camera, but to appraise the momentum and to exonerate the spirit of that place, well, it needed more to it. It needed the hand of a writer to assess its comeliness and symmetry. In an elevated mood I was having a momentary notion, that not many European women have had the opportunity to be birds of passage and enjoy a thoroughfare in its water the way my children and I were enjoying. Although many Europeans had been visiting China ever since, but they had never been to the spots we had been taken, not to speak of the reality of a calendar which denoted that we were in the 1980s. Feeling privileged I was happy and touched, embracing the lived past of a great people who were not altogether detached of their past.

My Birthday Cake Was Made of Trees and Wood

Li Po wrote on the beauty of the land, being very much close to nature. All his

> Like this green horizon halving the Three Peaks
> Like this Island of white egrets dividing the river
> Li Po, "On Climbing in Nanking to the terrace of Phoenixes"

poems render a big homage to the bloom and the natural alluring settings and environs.

It was the most striking scenery for me taking account that I was not raised in this environment. They indeed surprised me with their peculiarity and comeliness. Popping up from the depth of a lake, there I was looking at the small hills and islands that were like ornaments, and embodiment of Xuanwu Lake. Those forested islands were so special, so round, and so conic, as if they were shaped by an architect to grow up and stay in that shape. Tens and twenties of them, big and small, gave me the impression of birthday cakes. The trees and bushes surrounding the small pieces of earth stretched out of the transparent water, reminding me of the candles of a cake. My imaginative mind for once did not focus on the picture, since my husband and my children were all of the same opinion. And I made a wish, loud and clear, to make everyone on the boat to hear that I was to celebrate my fortieth birthday on one of these little bonsai islands. I baptised them on that day my "bonsai islands" so different out of everything I had encountered before. Bonsai is an art of cultivating artificially potted plants and trees smaller in actual size, thus a method to keep the trees dwarf. It started in China but the world recognised this art through Japan.

Nanjing was surrounded by green space. I do not know today how much vegetation and trees have remained since, not taking account of its beautiful parks, relying on the fact that the Chinese are pacing with giant steps to rebuild their country without undermining its natural beautiful surrounding to give way to modern and more economically derived and inspired projects. Those were the 1980s and Nanjing was yet this simple antique city hiding in it all the past vestiges of important and eminent history.

Each visit taught me something new on the Chinese character as a whole, enabling me to understand their behaviour and character by committing myself. The moment you showed curiosity and appreciation towards their commitments, they were encouraged to support you more with new and interesting information, thus rewarding your appreciation for having liked this monument – a garden or a sight.

This is how we were introduced to their temples and towers right at the heart of Nanjing.

My husband came to me one morning and said, "Be ready, since today we are invited by the delegation to have a historical tour of Nanjing temples and palaces, where no foreigners had set foot before since the First World War." My husband was overwhelmed and the excitement was for the tour I guessed, but the emphasis or the accent were more to the fact that we were being privileged by being again the first foreigners to visit a temple that no other visitor had had the chance to visit since the world war.

Our Chinese Guardian

We drove to the city which was a long way from our hotel like an hour drive. Something that I had not realised before, hence the more we were staying the more I was getting aware of the ways and the duration of our journeys. Something that I forgot to say is that from our first arrival to Nanjing we were introduced to a young man around twenty-eight years of age, a charming young man, to the utmost pleasure of my children, who were thrilled at his company. Conspicuously there was a very good communication established between them first due to the language, second because of our translator's disposition. He was designated to guide us all along our stay in the city. He spoke very good English. No need to say he became our mouth, our guide, and later on our friend. His name was Tsu. Mr. Tsu is good-looking, slim like most of his compatriots, middle height. A very timid person till the end, on all occasions he kept the same attitude, always reserved. He would talk only if necessary or if asked. That was his character even though that time I judged him, thinking it was due to the circumstances being always with foreigners, but many years later I discovered, when I met him in Switzerland, that was his true personality, reserved and shy. I must admit our trip had another charm due to his presence. He made our days easier translating and explaining on due time a dialogue between the employees or translating whole business sessions where important decisions were being discussed between both parties. He was honest and never tried by any means to choose sides. He was there to translate and that's what he did.

He was born and raised in Shanghai, and was working for this corporation. We had met him in Shanghai some six months prior to our visit to Nanjing, and since the chiefs of the corporations were working on the same programme, they had united their effort to convince my husband to start a joint venture in Nanjing in the pearl business, teaching and organising Chinese personals to the big production of pearl which was so scarce in those years. Unfortunately that's not the case today – bad marketing policy, better quality of pearls indeed, but too much quantity, which devaluated the price and the magic of pearl. It is very regrettable, nothing can alter this reality but we can prevent that disaster beforehand. Some ten years after our joint venture in Nanjing, quantity issue, controlling the output of pearl production in China, Japan and the South Sea, was the first and utmost priority of my husband. That's the main reason why we landed to Dalian, a very nice resort city on the China Sea, at the northeast of China. My husband meanwhile was endeavouring all his efforts to bring forth a coalition through the different corporations to bring forth all the big pearl dealers in the world to reconsider and restudy pearl industry in relation to world market demands. I will discuss of this issue and my trip to Dalian again after I go around my trips and visits chronologically, not to loose track of my stories. Notwithstanding between Nanjing and Dalian there is an interval of many years and a flourishing and promising joint venture. Now I must continue my visit and sightseeing in Nanjing before continuing my itinerary to Shanghai and then to Beijing to come back to Nanchang, the capital of Jiangxi Province.

Buddhist Temple

I was standing there in front of that old Buddhist temple fascinated and curious, my heart full of emotions.

I detached myself from the group and started to walk towards the profoundness of the temple. Giving a quick glimpse, my mind unwillingly was making a comparison with the Japanese temples with which I was more familiar. I was curious to see how much it resembled to the Japanese temples, since they were both Buddhist.

Buddhism and Its Role in China

I was being explained with short notes about the introduction of Buddhism and Buddhist art forms that reached China from India during the period of the Six Dynasties that had followed the prosperous Han Dynasty (206 BC-AD 220) from 400 years of unity. Chinese Buddhism and the fact that Nanjing was a centre of its propagation – especially the Mahanaya branch of Buddhism – had played an important role in shaping Chinese character and its civilisation as a whole. It had also a strong impact on the social and financial resources, becoming a source of inspiration and establishing impressive works of arts, new type of architectural spaces, temples, pagodas, and new types of gardens. Chinese Buddhism also widely influenced its neighbours, mainly Japan, who had a strong role in China's history. It was during the third century that Buddhist monks travelled to Japan, introducing the religion and its art and architecture, depicting different schools of martial arts. Of course Japan acquired the Zen teaching of meditation and contemplation and mostly retained the teaching of obedience, mainly to their emperors, who were going to become their living gods, till today with little nuance!

Temple without Spirit or the Ageless Spirit

That temple was beautiful more of a brick orange colour. It was not that big, but more profound. It smelled old and humid, propagating a putrid smell of wood lacer painting. It had resisted many century-long wars, but it was still there standing firmly and decisively on its decorative wooden columns in brick-red colour. There was a golden Buddha in its centre which was somehow different from the ones I had seen in Japanese temples that were mostly from wood in their natural colour, with no decorative symbols of art on or around it. Another thing which struck me is the fact that it was empty! I mean there was nobody in it, no burned candles, not even the sign of candles, which meant the temple was not in use, it was cold and hibernated. But now that I think back with some recoil, there were no cobwebs on its ceiling, nor dust on the altars. There were even big cushions of silk brocade where we sat with my children in the lotus style trying to contemplate. It appeared to me polished, clean, and ready to start a ritual action. During the Cultural Revolution, many temples and churches had been closed, practitioners persecuted. But fortunately, at the beginning of the 1980s, some Buddhist temples were allowed to reopen.

All they needed was to light the fuse and all would be illuminated at the speed of fireworks; trotting out of their hibernation, adjusting their demeanour to a right temperature and pulsation, thus yielding to the throb of the 21st century. Chinese had their philosophy born with and taught by Confucius and a very strong arm which is called "patience." With this arm they have maintained their ardour, their belief and their mettle.

My surprises and discoveries were not yet at their end in the city of Nanjing, especially when the chief of the delegation invited my husband and me to follow him in a separate ward of the temple in a sort of a backyard where the antique library of the monastery was. He told us this place was not visited by any foreigner since the Second World War and that we were some of the rare people authorised to visit it, including Chinese. Fearing dust and parasite, they were kept very minutely under serious supervision by the government. What I saw with my husband in that library was of immeasurable treasure and unaccountable human relic. He showed us books and calligraphy, which were written by scholars of some two thousand years ago. To enable their task they had to prickle their fingers to bring forth blood. At that moment I was not thinking of the human suffering but rather at the immensity of the work. My cheeks were burning out of excitement and my heart leaping in a kind of ecstasy. I was bent on the scrolls of those famous masters, Chinese letters all hand-written with big masters, poetry, essays, historical accounts, medicinal books, chronological data on wars and peace, different registration on eminent families, also there were many styles of calligraphy, I suppose of different periods and different schools. Of course, Chinese writing evaluated with the discovery of the paper and later on the ink. Their brush has a unique structure that allows it to hold ink in a reservoir (a solid black area in the brush). They are wrapped successively around a long central core of bristles of animal hair enhancing and playing a big role in the art of calligraphy.

Before we got into the room, our friend had told us not to touch the books. It was on our disposition to protect the parchments and papers from attacks of parasites, of course they were being treated and given extra protection against parasites and dust. When we came out of the monastery, everybody was looking at me to see what made me so pink with puffed cheeks, and eyes sparkling out of happiness and satisfaction.

Our next visit was a Ming palace, with its high walls and typical Chinese brick roofs and oval doors. Huge statues of mythological lions of some two to three meters high were on the main entrance to welcome the tourists. Nanjing had enjoyed its golden years under the Ming Dynasty, and there are many monuments of that period. What we enjoyed most of our exclusive and special visit was when after having made a tour in and around the rooms of the palace with their beautiful decorations, entire walls of rose wood screens lacked other designed with maidens of their relevant periods. Huge sofa beds were to the comfort of those beautiful concubines. Last but not least, we were taken in a very large hall where aligned Chinese style rosewood imperial chairs and tables all incrusted with mother-of-pearls and on the backseat there was a piece of marbled stones, like a soapstone – of some 30-40 cm finished with a very fine lace-like work engraved and incrusted all around. There were also scrolls of famous painters hanging on the walls with calligraphy of renowned poets and writers. The hall which I supposed was the throne hall, it was so extensive that the furniture and the statues were lost in it. But the better was yet to come: the chief of the delegation invited us to wear royal gowns of some 150-300 years old all in silk, other silk-satin brocades were mostly golden-yellow, white rose and royal blue with heavy hand embroidery. They had belonged to the ministers and notables of the Qing Dynasty as well as princesses and courtesans and nobles of the court (1644-1911). So we all started to put on the superb antique silk clothing honoured and more than happy to be allowed to wear them. Of course we have precious pictures of those important moments where for some minutes we felt like Chinese stately dignitaries. In French, the proverb concerning clothing says, "L'habit ne fait pas de moine," which means, clothing will not make out of you a monk. Germans say "Kleider macht leute," that is – clothing decides for your person – clothing is a powerful and ubiquitous way to communicate with the outside world. Indeed ours was a sort of game, yet when I recoil I know for sure that those royal clothings had given me definitely the pride of that rank. Each time I watch my picture with that antique clothing with its matching hat like a crown, I feel gratified having had the opportunity to feel imperious for a moment. Since a strongly lived moment is timeless, it is powerful and boundless.

For the next few days we were more in the working premises to enhance and endorse a successful business, the main reason of our itinerary. Through the years I had acquired the mastering of the pearl business and I could instruct and bring forth new students with the same teaching technique as my husband. Therefore I made myself more available on that intent leaving aside my curious and avid intentions to see more of the city's secret past. My children on the other hand were taken care by many baby sitters, not to forget our friend Tsu who, more than ever, was enjoying their childish but interesting company. Mr. Tsu discovered mostly the cassette-player of my son, then a teenager, who was in love with the music of Claydeman, a pianist accompanied by a symphony orchestra playing all kinds of soft music mostly composed by him. Till today we become nostalgic hearing his music which accompanied us all along our trip from Nanjing to Shanghai, like the background music in a film.

Before we left Nanjing and head to Shanghai, our corporation wanted to take us to some other sights of the city to see some of the pagodas, mostly the historical remain of the old stone wall, a remain from the Ming Dynasty during 1366 and 1388. I was told it was a wall encircling the city of over 33 kilometres averaging 12 meters high and 7 meters wide; it was built by more than 200,000 labourers. Made of bricks brought from five different provinces, each brick was stamped by the brick-master's name and the date. It is the longest city wall ever built in the world, about two-thirds of it still standing. We were standing at the top of it overlooking the city. I tried to keep cool not to sweat under the pressure of my emotions which were caught between the dancing breeze and my leaping heart.

On our way we stopped to Mochou Lake, in the western suburbs of the city. It was named after a heroine of the Liang Dynasty (502-557). It was a wonderful spot very attractive with many statues and water everywhere down from man-made brooks, cascades on top of huge rocks of porous origins; plum trees, peach trees and peony shrubs elegant and majestic with other exotic and funny plants, mostly bamboo weeds, all over and around the waters. Wooden patios surrounded the garden as for the walls. Something that amazed us all were their round door like opening giving to another entrance, other doors in the shape of a vase so different from European architecture. These enchanting entrances and refreshing mood of the garden pleased my children so much, who could find their happy moods once again after their visit to the high wall. To bring them out of that garden, my husband had to make use of his parental authority.

The following weeks, we had the chance to take our children to some famous gardens like Zhanyuan Garden and West Garden. As for the Water Pavilion, it was another enchantment for us. I do not know what my feelings would be today, some two decades after, when I know China's face is changing, so do my auspicious position and reverberate ventures. Notwithstanding, I was escorted by special cars. Big banquets gave me the feeling of eminence, gratifying me with all the courtesy and respects. So I felt very close to those monuments, very close to their whisper, to their song and poetry, to their folk stories, to their clothing and their food. There was no barrier between us. I was taken by their regards, their curiosity. In this way I intermingled exchange of knowledge, their sadness, worries, and aversions. All those issues engaged me even closer to their everyday reality, something which brought China and me to have the connivance to work hand in hand for mutual acquiescence, courtesy, and respect.

Song of Poet Li Po

Nearby the Linggu Temple, the temple that loomed the valley of the mountains, was the Linggu Pagoda. The pagoda itself was interestingly erect with so many stories, but most interesting and impressive was again a tangible token of the past that was to impress me again – a curved stone stele of a tomb of a monk Bao Zhi, who had passed away in the sixth century. The grave stone of some 2-3 meters high was engraved with a poem by the great poet Li Po, most loved and venerated poet of the golden age of Chinese literature, mainly poetry during the Tang Dynasty. The importance of the Tang Dynasty is significant in its importance to the political role to the feudalistic style dynasties, henceforth reuniting China after nearly 400 years of political unrest. The Tang Dynasty is also famous as the Silk Road period, where creativity, exchange of ideas and trade were encouraged and flourished. It was during the Tang period (at the beginning of the 8th century) in Sichuan that Li Po was born. Contrary to other Confucian or Taoist writers, he had not received a formal education. Despite this fact, he became a most beloved and venerated poet of his time, appreciated by the emperor,

Happily I walked the tavern down the line,
Passed an old drunk, holding a bottle of wine,
Do you not fear God?" was reproach of mine,
"said, Mercy is God's sign, in silence I wine and dine."

Secrets eternal neither you know nor I,
And answers to the riddle neither you know nor I.
Behind the veil there is much talk about us, why
When the veil falls, neither you remain nor I.

Omar Khayyam, Rubaiyat

the rich, and the poor society alike. He travelled all around China and made a meta-
phor of his person as a knight with a sword (dagger), writing his observations and
injustices within the empire. He was the poet of the people, free-spirited, close to
their aspiration, also close to nature; disdaining conventions around him, to bring
about and fulfil his desires through his strong pen. He was called the king without a
kingdom. He liked drinking, henceforth dedicated many poems on drinking. This
special characteristic reminds me of yet another world-renowned Persian poet, Omar
Khayyam, a great writer, mathematician, historian, and astronomer. Born in Nishapur,
today's Iran, in the latter part of the 11th century, he was the appointment of the Malik
Shah as his court's poet and assigned to reform the Muslim calendar. The *Rubaiyat*
(quatrain poems), his most famous work, was translated to English by Edward
Fitzgerald who lived in the 19th century. There are many parallels in the lives of these
two poets. Both were born on oriental land, both served their king, both were mystical
and wise, caring for the people, and sang the merit of the alluring nature: the moon,
the sky, the cosmos, rivers and mountains and the blossoms. Besides, they both loved
to dine and wine, privocating, fluttering and palpating the issue of the "Weal and the
Woe" which is reflected in their poems, they were both venerated and loved by their

From a pot of wine among the flowers
I drank alone. There was no one with me
Till raising my cup, I asked the bright moon
to bring me my shadow and make us three.
Alas, the moon was unable to drink
And my shadow tagged me vacantly,
But still for a while I had the friends
To cheer me through the end spring...
Li Po, "Drinking Alone with the Moon"

respective people ubiquitous till today.

First time that I came across Li Po's name was paradoxically in Japan, in one of my visits to Kyoto (old capital of Japan till the Edo Period). I visited many museums and temples in Kyoto, but this one was particular, especially to discover and learn the name of Li Po through two very precious paintings, one named "Peach and Plum Blossom Garden," depicting the story of the famous poet spending an evening with his cousins under peach and plum trees in full blossom. According to the description in the picture, night had just set in that scene, and moon (which was so much mentioned in Li Po's poems) outlines the pale blossom. Li Po and his cousins were eating and drinking rice wine and admiring the blossom of the trees, meanwhile it is said they were writing poems and comparing each other's work and rewarded with more wine.

Another painting which was hanged next to it is called "Golden Valley Garden." The scrolls were painted during the Ming Dynasty (1368-1644) by a famous painter Qiu Ying. These two scrolls were brought to Japan during the Edo Period (17th-19th century) and are kept there ever since, carefully cared by Chion-in Temple.

Therefore you can imagine my surprise to find a poem of Li Po that years ahead I had to come across his history and poems in a neighbouring country which had venerated an old Chinese writer.

The Shortest Way to the Crescent Is a Straight Line

During the following years we traveled to-and-fro many times to China. There we were calling at Hong Kong then continue on Shanghai and Nanjing. We went to Beijing more to meet high level government officials to validate a contract or for special permissions, meanwhile treating other businesses, or endorsing new ventures that were pending for certain reasons mainly financial that were lingering here and there. Contracts or joint ventures were not legalised unless they had the signature of the higher officers; it was a very careful and special arrangement. Each province had its autonomy to decide the way to handle, and with whom to handle his business. Once a joint venture is established within the city, it is the province which has the first responsibility, then comes in the authority of the city or prefecture and only then it is the central government in Beijing who has the last instance to comply to congruity of the agreements to arbitrate any endorsed contract signed in case of contention or disagreement from both sides. The central government is the only legitimate party to have authority on the debate and bring forth his final judgement. One thing we realised was that Chinese did not have the custom to write down contracts then, mostly they had agreements or verbal promises based on mutual respect and word of honour. To run after or idealise written contracts was an Occidental issue, adapted through the circumstances and need of the visiting party. They needed years and years of experience to come to understand the international rules based on realistic and pragmatic assessments and regulations; or in one word, the system based on and ruled for every international business. There was a mutual effort from both sides to endeavour in their mutual successes, to make some concessions, to come closer to the Chinese mentality without hurt feelings, nor provide the opportunity to major discrepancies, thus jeopardising major elements. The Chinese do not understand the mentality of the West, for example, to conclude business deals or great projects in a few weeks. Simply they can not understand this obsessive bargaining system. They have a long history behind them, an attitude, a reasoning, and a time frame somehow different from the West. They are very subtle and patient in their outlook and stance. They have the natural wisdom to act and decide with propitious and opportune timing, a manipulative attitude (for the West I suppose) playing at ease and indulging to their purpose. A very old philosophy of Taoism and Confucianism is behind their approach and frame of mind. They could read your mind; they could interpret your future and categorise your physiognomy to types or groups; especially the face. Some of the features indicate the conclusion, dissecting the form and interpretative expressions of the eyes, the mouth, the shape of the face to determine if you could be successful, reliable to work with, a strong character, honest, etc. Very intriguing and threatening, but this was their way.

In the West, this is portrayed differently. It is through more pragmatic and logical thinking and technology-bound methods. Analysis is done indiscriminately and arbitrarily to determine the character and ability of a person. In one word, more objectivity and a more rational attitude, though sometimes void of patience and more arrogant in their approach, sometimes ensuing prejudice, prevarication and pretence.

On the other hand, the Chinese relied on their contemplative power, and despite their fortitude and backbone towards intuition and manipulative thinking, and mostly their vehemence and potency on handling patience. Nonetheless, paradoxically their ardent desire and strive towards the attainment of Western technology in its totality was their utmost goal. And today we are leaving their attainment to that end to the most advanced technology.

Their subjective impute in finding the meaning in life, in intentions and desire was through controlling and observing the forces of nature, and implementing them, for the improvement of the physical life. For the objective and scientific mind this was very repelling and mystical, but for me it was fascinating and tangible! All these abstract notions and ideas, their analysis were a new approach, a new way for me to encounter. The wholeness of the cosmic reality startled me; a concept so new for me that I had to perceive its true meaning only after having studied some of the different concepts of their philosophy and their martial art, like Chi Kung and Tai Chi. Then after, for the first time it was possible for me to apprehend the Chinese concept of "balance" and "harmony" in relation to a healthy body and its accomplishment through mind and spirit.

My Acquaintances with Jade

I visited Nanjing on our way to Shanghai many times during the following years or to Nanchang, Jiangxi Province, which was another important crossroad regarding our business. No need to mention that along with our pearl business, we had many other interesting businesses, like dealing with carpets, vases of fantastic china, embroidery, gemstones, works of art in cloisonné, gold and silver exquisite pieces of art, notwithstanding statues and jewellery pieces in jade, the world did find the variety of these stones, so interesting and compelling, especially their inexpensive prices. I came across real jades in China and learned about them and their conspicuous history during my visits, and I learned a lot about their cost value, and energy value considering the science of the stone from an objective and subjective insights.

Jades Are Green and Multicolour and Unbounded Like Nature

Jade occurs in the form of jadeite, transversal jade and nephrite. Jadeite is a jade which crystallises in the form of grains and small elongated prismatic crystals. The most expensive and rare jade is the emerald green translucent jade or the "imperial jade" with shades of green from pale to deep, mauve, lavender. You can ferret out also white, brown, red, orange, yellow, grey, black, blue-green to green with white or light green traceries, also you can chance upon in pastel green with slight bluish cast incrusted with white veins. As for subjective values and energy values, I believe that stones which make part of our nature diffuse energies and each brings a certain specific help to the body and mind. Of course this is a subjective attribution. A very old science practised by different cultures such as by Aztecs and Mayan, jades represented a sacred stone, thus it was used for spiritual purposes. The same way as the science of herbalist or aroma therapy, they are more subjective and less scientific. You need to practise and have faith to feel the result. For example, I learned that jade when worn by the individual, enhances the realisation in one's potential of one's purpose in life. Jade is known as the "stone of fidelity" and "a dream stone." For example, a piece of jade placed under your pillow prior to your sleep will help you remember your dream. For some this may seem perplexed but for me they sounded true, having had experienced the energy of different stones in my life. I have dedicated a whole chapter about the healing power of gemstones and their different energy in another book dealing with health and beauty. Transversal jade is a variety of crystallise opaque green mass jade, due to its colour and opacity and more common, it is not highly quoted. As for its energy factor, it is said to help solve solutions through clear insight.

Nephrite is another stone of the jade family. It is composed of jade and actinolite, crystal, gold and pyrite, of course in the state of quartz crystal makes it even rarer. The colour ranges include olive green, green-grey, spinach green misty green, apple green, light green, brown-green, black cream, tan, blue-grey, and pink. It was venerated by Chinese emperors and also by priests who used the stone as material relics to venerate their gods. There are many statues and relics from those days in the Chinese museums. I also saw exquisite old Chinese jade statues of horses of one piece and maiden statues worth millions abroad in museums and fabulous jades with big stone-dealers, jades in hundreds of thousand dollars worth. Eminent Chinese poets have alluded many verses about jades and their beauty. For us in the West, the emerald, which is another green stone just like jade, is revered for its special green colour and translucent criteria. It is a form of beryl and crystallises in the form of prismatic crystals, terminated by stripes of pyramid-like facets. While the ones of much harder element and more intense green are most appreciated next to diamond, ruby and sapphire which are also classified as precious stones because of their hardness, colour and rarity. Emerald is known as the stone of successful love. It also provides stability bliss and loyalty to the bearer. Since I am alluding to stones, I can also mention the pearl criteria of which I am alluding all alone in this book.

The pearl is the queen of gems, while the diamond is being crowned the king of gemstones. They are grown in sea or lake or river in pearl oysters of different species. When an oyster looking for food inhales some pebbles or some group of sand or any other such material that could not be digested in its stomach, it starts to pour its nacre which embodies its shell. The nacre surrounding the intruder gives a certain form regarding the position of the intruder. Round perfect pearl is for the lucky diver, since you should know that till today the natural pearl or "la perle fine" is considered more genuine and more seek upon if they are big and round.

Pearl colours are categorised according to the sources of the pearl since not all have the same quality range, but nonetheless a white pearl is always the most classical, as well as the pinkish white and silvery grey colours. Then comes the Tahiti and South Sea pearls with their range of colours such as white, silvery, silvery-blue, black pearls, gold colours very rare too and my preference, grey, bluish-grey, champagne colour. The criteria of a nice pearl are: its size, colour, shape, cultivation, and blemishes.

Pearl signifies innocence, faith, and charity. It also enhances the bearer's wisdom and spiritual guidance. But in the case of pearls it also enhances good health. It is a very old medicine practised in China since hundreds of years till today in some areas. It is said to contain eight kinds of amino acids. Amino acids are the building blocks of all proteins, which are needed for the manufacturing of hormones, antibodies, enzymes and tissues in the body. Protein is the most important element for growth. It provides the body with energy and health enhancing long life.

My Second Baptism

My visits were of short stays of professional and business oriented. I must say as usual since I hardly visited a place with my husband and children, where business was not involved, even trips which were undertaken for vacation. Experience, flexibility in one's insight, concessions through acceptance were the main tools to deal when you do not eat your desired food, even if that food might look exquisite and tasty.

Very young, I was full of dreams, which were built-up and very deeply rooted in my adolescence. They became my heeds, flourished and pampered during my teenage period. Of course like everything in life dealing with many other issues, we encounter some difficulties either with people or the issues themselves. I do not deny that I was under the spell of my complacent dreams so I did expect some fulfilment of the path I had drawn, an itinerary created and nourished by a teenage girl. This is how you reason in your youth, sort of encourage your desires and then when they do not coincide with the pattern, there comes the wave of disillusionment. This is my situation with my husband and his trips, notwithstanding the fact that some of my friends would bite their lips out of envy, having the opportunity to see so many countries. I needed some maturity and acquiring some wisdom in order to appreciate the givings and mostly to understand that you cannot draw a life which was already drawn for you. You can make some complacency but never change the way. It is a one-way ticket bought by your parents and written by the cosmic order. They were told that the journeying of this ticket has to be fulfilled on due time and gratified through the blessing of life, the beauty of its unbounded nature, then to learn gradually about the good and the bad, the disappointments, the successes and the defeats, the knowledge of the ugly and the comely, the poverty and richness; last but not least, about deceit, treason, and jealousy. All these I had to encounter on my life's ticket. Giving a long thought about it, considering that only ten percent of humanity can boast of having received the gold ticket while the silver, copper and iron were divided in the remaining group. A ratio which can be subjective and cannot be concluded hastily. To experience dreams is good! Will is what makes us to go forward. Desires and belief need to be maintained and hope is the essence of life as for illusion is our shadow which straightens under the strong sunrays to reappear at sunset to sit on your side to make you one with your daily reality.

Time is magic and it engulfs in it all the wisdom of this world. Experiences give insight to your life and make you understand that some of the realities push you towards concessions to be able to ram in the river of your karma. So it was like a "take it or leave it" attitude, so I took it! The result was enchanting and conspicuous. My commitment was well established, my determination at hand and my positive character put to work. To activate all these I needed new, constant sources of energy. That was on my way too, all I needed to do was to be consecrated and ordained towards that end in order to make the utmost out of it.

Drawn in my inner self, looking for some answers about life and my encounters, weighing the givings of our lives and the destinies with which we had to abide, but as soon as I heard my husband's foot steps, they shook me up from my state of deep thoughts, dressing my reality of the moment tangible and lively, grasping those gratifying moments before they become the illusion of a lifetime. He announced that we were invited to a big banquet and many big chiefs from Shanghai were to be there too. I was getting used to banquets, having experienced so many of them which were exquisite. Nanjing is hospitable, as well as all the other cities that I visited. Orientals are generous and hospitable people. I can conclude my statement through the different visits I encountered.

At the banquet, the chief had introduced new rural reforms which were working out and making an immense change in the system, thus engaging new order in the economics of the country. Due to this reform the communes were being dismantled and returning to the individual farming family as the basic agricultural production unit. Pearl was quoted as an agricultural production, yet despite these big changes within the country, many options were going to be very decisive on our business for the years to come. It also meant that the big cities like Shanghai, Nanjing and Beijing were not going to be able to interfere directly on our business, at least we were sure of one thing that was the step of our future and the imminent, newfangled and redesigned business transaction for the coming consequential years to live up to and pattern ourselves upon. We could purchase directly if we wanted to from the fishery or the agricultural domain, keeping abreast of or supporting them to make individual households sign contracts which would specify an output quota and allocate certain plots to their use; or the specified output quota would be turned over to the collective and sold to the state at the fixed base price, above quota production it may be sold directly in rural or urban markets. And after a few years after exactly in 1988 that's what happened in our business.

All this news was ambiguous and so quick that was creating some confusion and indigestion during that gorgeous banquet full of all kinds of Chinese food. I had hardly seen before and could not recall their names or imagine in any other restaurants in Europe or in the US. They were done with so much delicacy and art. Green, yellow, red, and orange vegetables cut and designed in lace-like artful works, so appetising. Inviting pastries were mostly prepared with rice and honey, broiled or deep-fried in a certain mastery way to give the dough a special form. Centre pieces garnished with raw vegetables used as decoration, thus giving the form of different animals, so beautiful and palatable. All these displays and presents taste and mastery of the culinary art. Savoury dishes would always tempt you first with the eyes. Chinese lavish artful table bears comparison with Roman's and Greek's, which according to history books, some two thousand years back, they had an inclination and love and a whole philosophy towards dextrous and artful eating, accompanied with preposterous and ludicrous manners, to be able to eat more and more, to satiate the eye and the pleasure of gourmandise eating. The Epicurean school, a philosophy to eat and be merry, is a good example of their attitude in those times.

Chinese food is easy to digest, therefore you would eat slowly and taste everything gradually, which would hold your greed and anticipate your gourmandise. And speaking of healthy and balanced food, it is unexcelled. The only thing, which bothered me that I had to face almost in all banquets, was the drinking part of the ceremony. Thank God, being a woman played a big deal to halt and minimise detriment to become tipsy, an act that would make me merry. When I was new in China I was very attentive not to exaggerate with the number of glasses. Besides they never or rarely pour drink to me, since for them in the Chinese social group or protocol, drinking was a manly behaviour. Fine virtuous women would not drink. I did not understand or make a relation of the moralist and bad in this context. Who was the good woman for them, and what were her qualifications? Thank God, I was considered the different woman, coming from the planet Europe, a faraway land called Switzerland where women in society had a different treatment indeed.

Therefore, inclining to this reality, I was left the choice. But this new, off-the-wall situation was dubious, because each time my hosts were running across this unorthodox reality, nonetheless my wine cup was taken care of, I mean refilled. The only impediment was my husband John who was always there watching me with some tease and concern, actuality out of fear seeing me getting tipsy and some times very quickly, especially on hot weather, and after business cessions dealing and concluding important and pending discussions. Well, I must also say that the other way was also right. I mean my husband, who unlike me, did not like to drink at all. He only drank when he was obliged, either to animate a friendship or celebrate a fulfilled contract. So each time we were in such situation, I had to watch over him, by reminding him not to be intemperate or overplay, especially when he starts getting red like a tomato and sweating like he is sitting in sauna. So our mutuality was like everything else, taking care of each other in arduous moments to save our inconveniences mutually. But unfortunately sometimes events speed up spontaneously and when you like drinking, like in my case, you are under its spell. So that was my situation that day, on that gorgeous banquet, a wonderful reminiscence of cherished moment in time.

Our table was a very long one. We were about thirty people, me being the only woman guest. As a respect I was sitting beside the Shanghai deputy minister, who, I must admit was the most gallant man I ever met in China to that day. He was very tall, a big man of around fifty of age, not a single white hair, almost white skin with big almond eyes of very profound, intelligent gaze, with kind looks. I looked around me and eyed all the guests one after the other. They were all dignitaries, strange faces, only a few people of our group were there that night, including our precious and mostly treasured on that evening – our translator Mr. Tsu. Notwithstanding my husband and I were the only foreigners, something that did not bother me anymore. I felt good and comfortable surrounded with these people, who were not my people, indeed being from another planet, the other continent, but I felt good! The fact that we were close but not the same did not modify my feelings. They did not seem to me different at all. They were unlike any other VIPs in their stance, who were modest and simple. I suddenly felt at home happy and relaxed. I felt an appeasing mood full of attention and heed to please the guests of the party. They cared about us, they wanted to learn more about our concept and behaviour. We were a live example of what the other continent was. Their business was important indeed, but for that precise moment they wanted to show their Oriental hospitality, without any pretence, almost a candid curiosity trying to overhaul and understand us with respectful and accepting intentions of the difference that was so much emphasised very probably to enhance and underline a tightened friendship.

It is amazing and strange when I think back of those moments in time. In those moments I could grasp the relation created and lived between different races, strong relation of love, attraction, marriages between Eurasians. Because when there is real respect and love, you will not see the difference.

I looked towards my husband, who seemed cheerful and relaxed, in a high mood listening to different conversation through translation and sometimes through guessing, making use of his limited Chinese vocabulary. In any case after an hour, when a few glasses were already emptied, they were all going to speak a new language, Sino-English created just for the occasion. Considering that the effort was not only from our side, it was bilateral, me too trying to manipulate, and memorise some instant Chinese words in addition to our vocabulary, as an extra effort to understand each other! The chiefs were becoming more friendly, and less tense, seeing our simple behaviour and friendly attitude towards the group. The table started to get very animated and our deputy minister was pouring my glass, with utmost respect from a chief. Meanwhile my husband had forgotten, for a while, to watch and count my cups. Out for once I was left free, really free, to drink at my ease like a mature woman, taking her own responsibility in front of the running danger. If danger there was! It was not in the quantity of drink I was taking with my dinner that worried me most but the quality of the drinks.

What I mean is that all the time they were changing the course of the drinks. We were drinking Chinese rice wine, very sweet to my taste, then change to another wine from another province, a wine appreciated for being very dry and with a pungent smell, then to go ahead with beer – a product and pride of the province – so how to refuse all of this panoply, deluge of drinks, which were dancing all around our table, each one of us had a waiter serving to, so there was no way to escape or say No. The moment I was engaged into a conversation, in a fraction of time, already the glass was refilled. I could not even pretend drinking if each time my glass was really filled up. My only way to escape the drastic situation was when I started sipping water now and then, to dilute the drink in my stomach. Since there was no way I could prevent the waiter to refill my glass on the table.

Oh yes, yes but not like this. I can mix up the white and the red wine, indeed but not the yellow, the pink, the beige and the white. Well I started calling the name of all saints and Jesus to help me not to get drunk and to play my role of the dignified lady of the table. I had the hard and difficult responsibility to represent all my like, not only I had to play the role of the emancipated woman, but also I had to animate a very difficult topic going from the changes in China, my views and my impressions and my critics which they listened very carefully. They sometimes shake their heads, some-times leave a big laughter, and most of the time let a little exclamation, which I could not guess if they meant angry or happy about the pronounced feelings and reasoning. My situation reached Tao point that I started to make them resemble to some of my friends and even one of them to my uncle. Of course, when I declared this reality to them, there was such a big laughter that I regretted my honesty and was starting to shake down my legs. I was not feeling my voice starting to tremble and having some difficulty to follow up the conversation. Thanks to the dialogues which came to my rescue since they could not guess my uneasy drastic situation created through my dizziness since I was afraid to stand up fearing that I could not straighten my body to be able to walk. Suddenly I had the genius idea to soak my napkins in the glass of water to sweep my face with it and to refresh my neck and my temples. Since I was well-oiled, I was sweating like hell. No matter how strong the ventilators were running, still the room was hot, appeasing the hot taste of our food but not helping my palpita-tion or stopping the dizziness in my head. Thank God I had no nausea yet. I think water did help my stomach to balance the sugar converted to acid and the alcohol to sugar, but on the other hand, the quantity of water made my stomach a balloon, pushing so much on my diaphragm which was in turn pushing and narrowing my rib cage, my waist got so tight that I thought the zipper of my dress was to give up. Well, it is better to have fears in such situation that live a worst nightmare with people whom you just met and maybe you will never meet them again. Well, I must say recalling this event I have a smile on my face to the fact that I managed the situation with grace and tact. My husband was thrilled at the complements to my person. The chief had told our translator that I had adorned and embellished their table that evening and that my suggestions were most gratifying and proficient. He promised to visit us in Switzerland to bring forward a mutual success in our business endeavours. He was very thankful of our achievement and hoped better and broader understanding towards their differences – something that touched me a lot coming from an eminent man, a high ranking government personality.

I was taken into this incessant hospitality. I had to accept the game not to disfigure or impair the trend of mood or undermine the reality of my status belonging to the other continent's female, having in mind that they would take for granted my different attitudes and concepts with a strong prejudice at the bottom of it. Our inclination towards wine in this part of Europe was customary. For us to drink wine if not every day but most of the days was accepted and ordinary. Therefore to accentuate and indicate our custom and wine liking, which more than a custom, was a personal issue. I started telling them a childhood reminiscence, an event to show them clearly and elegantly, my natural inclination towards it. Despite wine is always attributed to be a male beverage, Bacchus, the wine god of the Roman mythology, was also a man. An antique reality which could not befriend to my *yin* gender. Now all ears were atten-tively promoted towards my end, eyes were all pointing at my person. Some had an amused look, some were open-mouthed. Nonetheless there was a general curiosity, since I was disclosing something of my private, even if that private was long time ago. For them anything said about our lives was interesting and terribly acclaimed. The same way anything said or brought about their own lives would have had the same impact on me.

Mr. Tsu was most far-reaching in earnest in his role of interpreter. Very seldom had I seen him like this, with a face glowing and timid at the same time. A kind of pride could be read on his face which I had not seen before. I looked at him to know the real reason of his sudden happiness, but already he was looking on the other side, trying to explain through translation, once again to some of the inquisitive faces who wanted to attend by all ears and hang on my words.

Thank God and why not thank Bacchus for taking care of me in those precious moments without giving way to another analysis. I dropped the first words with a soft and singing voice, like an actor in front of his spectators.

"One day," I went on, "my father, my younger sister (that time seven years old and me around fourteen) and I were having lunch at home, my two other sisters and my mother were away on a short trip. We were being served and attended by our nanny who had gone through a painstaking effort to prepare lunch and dinner during my mother's absence to make us feel happy with all our exigencies and food we cared and favoured most. So it was one of those days, she had prepared chicken accompanied with French fries, a lunch that my younger sister and myself were fond of. My father on the other hand, seeing this nice food, asked our nanny to open a bottle of wine, who executed right away. I have to say that my father was a very good wine connoisseur. He could recognise a good old wine, describe its particularity and distinction. He could indicate the year of the wine and the millesime and its renown. He had a cave full of French, Swiss, and Italian wines especially. He was a collector of French Bordeaux wine and had kept aside Bordeaux wines with the year of our birth date. We were five children, so each one of us had that privilege that we cherish till today. Some of those wines wait to be opened for especial occasions, such as high school diplomas or engagement or any such important event to be celebrated. As we had at hand all kinds of wine kept also in our big and spacious dining room to facilitate the service and the momentum." All this details translated by Mr. Tsu was creating a more friendly atmosphere, which was encouraging me in my eloquent storytelling. Nonetheless trying to diminish the furnace on my cheeks, which were getting so hot that I thought the wave of its heat would kill some of the mosquitoes whizzing around my head.

"The open bottle laid on the table, my father started first to pour in his glass. Making use of the wine language, he started describing the wine which had a good appearance, had a backbone and depth, nice body. It's a cuvee, he would go on adding, which is dry and earthy, in another word elegant, not floral neither grapey, rather hearty. After a while noticing the sparkle of my eyes, he had a gesture and leaned towards me and said, 'I can pour your cup only half, since you have school in the afternoon, therefore you should be careful with the amount.' While filling my glass he started lecturing on the quality of the wine. He went on adding, 'It is a very good wine, I want you to taste. It is a Château Neuf du Pape, not a very heavy one, which goes well with our dish. You should always choose a wine which corresponds to your taste first, but it has to correspond the food too. For example with fish, we rather take a rich white wine and with meat red wine, with good elegant hearty wine which has depth and is dry; with foods which are rather with some kind of sauces, you can either choose a floral fresh spicy or perfumed or floral red wine or a rose wine which you could drink cold (years after all rose had to be the choice of my husband, not because they were easier to digest but because he could drink them cold).' Almost at every wine drinking my father had to show us the quality through the language of wine with the right words, to express the smell and taste and colour of the wine. Learning the language of wine he would go on telling us, 'It will enable you to communicate your own perception of the wine. It is a refined art of class, which you acquire through experience; an issue which is so personal. Discovering the aroma and flavours and sharing your assumptions with others is such an experience.' added my father.

"My palate was appreciating every sip of the wine, and meanwhile answering to my father's criteria, who seemed very satisfied of his daughter's answers.

"My father looked at his watch and said, 'I must take a leave, children, you have some time left, but do not be late to go to school, now I have to leave.' He kissed us on our cheeks and left.

"I was left with my younger sister on the table to finish our food, and to run to school. Our nanny was already in her room to have some rest.

"In French we have a nice proverb which says 'Le chat est parti, les souris dancent' – 'When the cat is gone, mice dance on the floor.' My father left and I wanted to gratify myself with wine. I grabbed the bottle of wine still half full and started to fill my cup. In order to buy the silence of my sister, I also filled her cup, who was most happy of my gesture not because she especially cared about wine, but because at that age they did not like to be omitted or left out of any circumstances or event to be considered young and be kept away of experiences. This is true almost with every child, and my sister did not make any exception, neither did I. Seeing that my sister liked the wine, I poured her one more glass and another for me. Now we were getting merry, I was seeing myself a heroine, my sister Malvina thrilled, to be accepted and make part of the ceremony. I was flabbergasted seeing the bottle emptied, thank God I had not lost my reflexes even though my knees started trembling and my cheeks getting red hot (I almost wanted to add like now), but I did not want to give way to comparison. We started laughing for any silly talk or any gesture. We were flying! We were tipsy and topped under the influence of wine. Of course that time I did not know that giving free rein to the regale of two or three glasses of wine, I had indulged myself this funny situation. My act was naive even though I knew that one could get bibulous through drink. But the truth is that I had met beforehand.

"No matter what, I did take the direction of my school which was a five-minute walk from our house. My sister was jumping and getting emotional. We reached the school's gate, a huge wire gate. It was closed. This was an indication that we were late. But why did nanny not tell us? Most probably she was asleep! Yet in my tidily situation, my logic was awake since I could tell my sister to rush to her class. She obeyed. She was merry, laughing and running towards her class. Till today I do not know what was the result of her aftermath in the classroom." I stopped and took a long breath, and I realised that my story awakened my fellow delegation and with it their curiosity. The effect of the wine and its repercussions through my storytelling was playing its magic; I was trilled. Then I stopped little bit to give a chance to my friend Tsu to follow up my story in his translation. Their faces now were more close to the table as if trying to understand my words or maybe to anticipate my story through my gestures, an assessment that encouraged me to continue. I went on saying, "I took the stairs of my school to climb to the third floor.

"I remember as of today, how light and free I felt, laughing all by myself. I had burning cheek and eyes which were on fire, my temples started to throb. As for my mind, I am sure it was in a state half asleep and half awake, under the influence of the alcohol. I reached the front of our classroom, the door was already closed. I knocked the door again, stood there at the threshold and looked around fearlessly and without any guilt conscious, laughing and bubbling some excuses, the habit of the subconscious mind I suppose. My teacher came close to me, looked at me and noticed the unthinkable! He pulled me out of the class and said, 'I see that not only you are late but are in a very bizarre attitude. I know your mom is not here, but again your attitude is incorrigible. Now at this instance go wash your face, take a round through the school-ground and when you think you can find your spirit, come back.'

"Till today I do not know if this event was mentioned to my mother or father, but thank to my wonderful teacher and his understanding, I was not punished for my act. I do not know either what or how my sister came out with her tippling situation. But when I had questioned her the next day on how she managed with her class, she was flabbergasted and my question was out of place because she added none of the things I was asking she could recall of. I was amazed too, was this a joke or was I dreaming or making it up? Days went by, my mom came back to find her loved ones and the next day around lunch time, she told me that nanny had drunk half a bottle of wine all by herself during her absence and that made them laugh for many, many days. Well, this was a long time ago, to evince and demonstrate once again my appreciation for wine was both hereditary through genes, and through the teaching of appreciation. My father, among many other things about life, had taught me and bestowed the curiosity, the novelty and heed to love and appreciate life's giving, in one word, to have 'la Joie de Vivre'."

Now my Chinese friends reached closer to the table edge, this way to get closer to my voice, trying to make the parallel with my person. They all started to laugh and shook their heads not knowing in which direction to judge. They could not really picture the scene since some of them had never left China in those years. It was not really a social concern, they were satisfied by the recitation, the same you hear in a novel or a fairy tale; in this case the only difference was that the protagonist was herself telling her story. As for the moral and the message of the details, no body was interested. They did not want to engage in that direction. What's most important for them was my humour and my company. I had no pretence and they had no preconception, so at that moment they were like docile children listening to a friend telling them about such an event. Later on Mr. Tsu added that they felt very concerned of my story, especially the fact of having to share with them a happy moment of my private life. They enjoyed my story so much he went on telling me, happy and content mostly the contingency, reminiscence alluding to my father and sister.

Chinese are very family-oriented, for them unity of the family is very important, and in my story, more than the wine, they were most impressed and concerned with my relation to my father and sister. Well this is true for all of us. Thousands of people watch a film, but everybody gets what he wants from that film. Sometimes they are subjected to the main theme, sometimes the events promoting or engaging to that subject. Well that night during that banquet I had a similar situation.

We went to our hotel. I laid down on the bed, to wake up the next morning with the aroma of good coffee, mixed with the smell of bread and butter, inviting and appetising. I opened my eyes, the sun was almost down on my bed, caressing my face and my arms, inundating myself with the sensation of fulfilment and gratification. Even though I had a little headache, yet I knew that was nothing compared to the rewarding and pleasant venture I had experienced that evening and I had made an all out effort not to succumb, and I had not. Everybody was happy, my guests as well as my friends. Mr. Tsu, when I met him in the hall of the hotel, was happy, but timid and reserved as usual. No need to say that I did not allude to that evening, because everything was said and emotions expressed like ever before. Or maybe to be honest towards my subjective feelings, my inner voice was telling me something. And my subconscious was right. The ensuing moments were to prove what my conscious mind was refusing to admit. Yet no matter how hard I tried not to question him, the answers had come to me. My herald (Mr. Tsu) was standing there very politely with a package in his hand. Very politely and gently he handed it to me. I was startled and at a loss, could not guess the content of the package. I grabbed it and tried to open it. Now curiosity was getting hold of me. The moment was very impartial, objective and unprejudiced. "Oh," I said; seeing my pair of shoes at a loss, I was coming down on like a bolt from the blue and being caught on the wrong foot. Taken aback and speechless looking again at my shoes, now out of the package, I could not and in any case stay impartial. My mind would rebuke me if I dared telling him – why on earth are my shoes with you, since my unbiased senses, on the spur of the moment realising the scene, hushed on my memory. I remember of course not the details, since late that evening my conscious mind had retracted and drawn back under the spell of the drink, letting my nature free to act and react to the comfort of my body, henceforth I had taken out my shoes during late hours of the party, consequently and having come to the hotel leaving behind my "pair of shoes"; my long gown hiding my bare feet from discrete eyes.

Next I have a nice adventure again with my trip to Nanjing, but this time we were heading to Shanghai especially to Suzhou which was a small town (today a big city), one hour distance from Shanghai by train. Suzhou today is an important market, producing and selling pearls to the tourists visiting Shanghai.

In Nanjing and its area, pearls were being sold not as strands but by weight, the way you would sell rice to a new market. But rice is a necessity, while pearl only a luxury item!

Corporation had opened another pearl factory and we had to go there to meet the new employees and the staff, hence to co-operate in organising the correct procedure of the factory. I was nostalgic a little bit, not being with my children since we had walked the same itinerary with all three of them some years ahead. I was hearing the echo of their laughter and their enthusiasm.

We stayed some times there dealing and working with the same group which was a rare incident, since with other corporations, every now and then some of the personals would be gone, others changed with another representative. When asked, we could not get a clear answer, as if we were hitting to a wall. For us this attitude was not well apprehended, alluring to this reality our disposition and concept compared to the Chinese is very direct and transparent, therefore their perspective was not well understood. Of course with time we were getting used to their personality and acquiescence, through passivity a smooth friendship was paving.

By the way, the secret of friendship is interests based on understanding and sharing, where appreciation, common view and faithfulness are the key contributors to the enhancement of that friendship. This is how friendship is explained by Khalil Gibran in *Prophet*. Born in 1883, he was a poet and a philosopher who lived most of his life in USA, France, Italy, and Greece. He passed away in 1931 in Boston. He sang human character and moods. A mystical man who loved beauty and saw beauty even in death. He was named prophet because of the depth of his subjects.

Your friend is your needs answer
He is your field which you sow with love and reap with
  thanksgiving...
Seek him always with hours to live
For it is his to fill your need, but not your emptiness...
For in the dew of little things the heart finds its morning and is
  refreshed.

Khalil Gibran, *The Prophet*

My Second Initiation

One day, my husband, along with his fellow translator Mr. Tsu, came to me and suggested that we go to Nanjing with the corporation, since there was a business to be dealt directly with the corporation in Nanjing. He went on saying, "After that we could go for another sightseeing, something that you will enjoy." Since the answer to the question was already there, and the plan well established and assessed, all I had to do was to be co-operative and affirmative and to say "yes" to show my contentment to their prepossessing programme, order of events scheduled and apprehended by men.

Next day early in the morning, I was well awake to encounter my new day, to hail another happy adventure, having in mind that however well planned itinerary, the unexpected could surface from our ways. Not a day looked alike, I hardly had time to think of the past. Already I was involved in the present with its new events. As for the projected future it had to carry the magic and the mood that embodied all of my trips, therefore our future was on the pink and promising taken care by itself. It seemed to me that when I was there in China, I entered another dimension, the past, the present, and the future would intermingle, notwithstanding my timetable was ordained by China and not made in Switzerland; as if I was in a bulb of time machine, cut of every reality, excluded of the outside world and of every other existence. There existed only China, the pearl, and I.

I was on a planet indeed. China with a selective group of Chinese personals, I was introduced to the exclusive and advantaged where nature was orderly and comely, surrounded of nothing comparable unless by itself, reminding me of other sights, having the same allure and comeliness! Notwithstanding that was a reminder; not once

I was angry or disappointed because I did not have to analyse or to compare. I was attracted by the novelties and the remarkable achievements and mostly by their civility and their friendly treatment and attention.

To visit and explore is such a pleasure in that environment, where they reward you in many ways. Perceptive and sagaciousness serve to consider your honest friendship and devotion. Their appreciation is to make you feel that you are important without any superlative, nor make you feel that you are conceited or they are condescending. Feelings run out with contentment, there was a mutual mood of understanding to bring forth success that both parties were looking forward. To water all these moments, we were hosted through lavish exotic food, inundated through generosity and politeness. What a hospitality!

I was almost ready to go down to the dining room to take my breakfast, my husband was already to his business. I felt a little tired that morning. The heavy weather and the dampness of the atmosphere were bothering me. I was not used to this kind of climate, and no matter how much effort, I was exhausting to preserve my body from the target of that condition. But apparently that morning the harmony between my body and mind were not in place; and the result was not rewarding either for myself or for my husband, who did sense my uneasy mood. He asked to postpone the trip for the next day, but my response was negative to his kind solicitude. We were already out of our country for five weeks. I was starting to miss my children, even though I was calling them from now and then. I had exceeded the deadline of our schedule; I wanted to carry out our business as planned. Therefore I made an all effort to continue the itinerary no matter what. Furthermore I did not want to compromise the mutuality and the coherence that had been established with our corporation, with which we dealt during our frequent visits. Above all, I was not sick, but homesick; I had a kind of fatigue and exasperation due to a lack of my daily comfort. But thank God, I was a robust woman. Situations like these did not linger with me very long. I would take over very quickly. I would be mesmerised by the quick shift of my moods from the turndown situation.

Now we were in a minibus to Nanjing. It was an old Chinese car, rather comfortable. In any case in those days you could not expect more, nor did I want more, having in mind that the exterior richness was not an indication or a must to influence or promote a rank or a situation; either a contribution to enhance your business deals or in our case friendship burst out of business. Chinese people in general are modest people.

This comes from their education, a Confucian-based learning which expresses tolerance, patience, and humbleness, next embodied with the contemporary socialistic feelings being satisfied with what they had and not look to get enriched. For me in those days they were modest souls, acting and working for the same goal, to come out of poverty and to bring their country on the rank of the powerful nations. Over and above all I even felt somehow unobjectionable and innocuous. I could see a transparency in their expressions, wide-eyed and candid. You might think I am getting emotional or rather overwhelmed throughout my feelings, but no! I truly felt so. I cannot say I was deducing or assumed from my conversation. I could engage a conversation only with a few people. Either I had to go through our translator or to use my hands to express my thought, and if all the other means were not enough, I used the eyes, which were even stronger than pronounced words, since they burst either from the heart or the head; in any case they were the true expression of the soul and you could not go wrong with it by drawing to a close. And exactly on such moments where feelings are expressed, you could seize and carry out, no matter what they want to express or demonstrate. Most of the people in the streets that I met were candid people, some ignorance embodied their world, but among these groups I did meet also conspicuous persons whose memory I still cherish till today.

But as I am alluding about luxury and comfort, well, maybe the luxury of that time was to have an air-conditioner in the car which indeed was the utmost luxury for me, for us, since to drive in that heat would have been a real nuisance for all the passengers, six in number including our driver.

The sun was hitting the windows of our car with such a force, each time becoming more and more aggressive. But thank God, advanced technology with its air-condition was not on odds outdoing with it. Notwithstanding its white luminous ray whose heat was being reflected and refracted back and forth from the surface of our car, to be lost somewhere on the pavements, hence trying to spread on trees, to satiate its thirst trying to lick the dews which had been on the leaves of the trees. The passers-by and the diverse people walking on the streets, most of them sitting on their bikes, were the first morning target of the rays. They were inflicted to bear the blazing heat, which were entangling and scrambling by subjugating them to heavy breathing and abundant perspiration – an affliction which reminded me of a similar situation years back, coming out of our gym classes.

We reached Nanjing late evening. Some of the times cha was a very efficient drink to combat heat, thus to bring the body heat in equilibrium with the outside heat. On our way we had a small incident – nothing serious, but rather special in its alluring condition.

Crossing a land by car is always more interesting, enhancing you the opportunity to watch and observe details more easily, letting you enjoy different panoramas, such as rice fields, piled cocks of hays, water all around extended like never I had seen before, bushes of different forms, panoramas of different mood and sight. A dry spot would give way to a green vegetation of fertile prolific fields of different shades. You do not understand how and why in an interval of some twenty km drive you could have such contrast of aridity then, again everything so bounteous and green; massif mountains encircling whole regions, thus making a natural protective wall. I was silent all the time. My husband was busy talking and discussing some socio-economic topics with two of his major personals who happened to speak good English. There was another woman in the car, therefore as the custom wanted, we sat near each other at the rear of the car, leaving my husband with men at the middle and front of the car. As I said earlier, time had no place in our schedule. We were their guests and they were leading our time, our moments and our days. If I had to consider their time with my Swiss timing, I do not even want to think of the outcome; so I was well aware of my space and the unaccountable time. I was happy, and felt I was in a cradle with the car's movements. A very light and nostalgic mood was caressing me. My morning mood was already adjusted and seized by the curiosity of our trip, ensuing the balance between my body and mind.

Our driver, Mr. Young, a very curious man, was reacting with spontaneous gestures of pride at my happy exclamations about the beauty of the land. Each time I expressed bending in front to show the details to my husband, who, between us, was not interested at all of the scenery outside, who rather preferred the inner world with which he was conferring.

But things changed when we reached a lake! At its first revelation I thought it was a rather extensive wide pond, owing to its very shallow edges and full of mosses; but right away I was told it was a lake and a large one, with many islands like sections. Crowded with locust trees and poplars, willow trees were bending their waist till the depth of the lake, their pliant branches were swimming on the glass-clear water of the lake, thus refracting their beauty to the infinite cosmic space, henceforth refusing to hide their beauty in the depth of the water. They were being caressed from time to time by the air currents coming across the North.

Now we were out of our car and walking along the lake, to get closer to this beautiful scenery. As usual I was overwhelmed and taken by the beauty of the place. My husband was already seeing the place as a future investment spot for tourist attraction, with motels and restaurants around the lake, to be enjoyed by everyone. Well that was his way of seeing and making use of nature's unequalled beauty. Of course, he was projecting his idea, foreseeing a prosperous future for the land, which was more business oriented simple hypothesis burst from his heart and business-minded personality. Nonetheless I did not have the same perception or bore his concept. Apparently I was not unanimous in the group, since I was left alone on the objective and plan, because the enthusiasm of the group was so high that I had to give up any argument, not to deter my inner peace and joy. We continued our walk along the coast of the lake to come to another breath-taking sight that surprised me with its exquisite beauty that left me bewildered and mesmerised for a moment. I was seeing for the first time in my life water lilies or lotuses that big, in their real dwelling. They were out of reality, enigmatic, sitting there on the surface of the water, enthroned on big, almost round leaves of dark chlorophyll colour. The lotuses were of three colours: first I noticed the immaculate white colour, then a pink one smiled to my face, and very far almost untouchable in the depth of the lake, there was a "nymph" – this is how I called those lotuses of very dark purple colour as large as 30 cm in diameter. Ephemeral flowers, which would hatch and blossom to live a short life span of only twenty-four hours. Words had no force to be expressed orally what my emotion were to acquaint. I was mystified; feelings were strangling me; a terrible desire, an envy, was obsessing me. A momentum to get hold of those lotuses, to enable me to touch them, feel their soft velvety petals and to smell their fragrance, as a rapture, a challenge of encounter, like Sindibad's fascination while encountering the necromancy of the ravishing flower. Never had I seen a water lily this large and of these colours. Their leaves underneath had covered all of the surface of the lake with its natural boundaries made by the presence of porous stones so familiar and ample in the area, walling small lakes, one into the other. Those were sections and portions of unbounded beauty – a decoration, a sight that nature had designed where mankind could only imitate. Now I was silent. I had seen indeed many comely natural spots, such as the Swiss Alps and its evergreen fields of unequalled beauty which would rapture your curiosity, a beatitude towards nature's alluring, necromantic and especially tidy beauty. The European chain mountains are the Alps, the highest summit being the Mont Blanc (4807m), next Mont Rose, the Matterhorn, and the Jungfrau. Their exquisite beauty enveloped in a heavy coat of fir trees. Those mountains are the source and life bearer of many rivers, such as the Rhine and the Rhone, and next to their feet overlooking the emerald green sparkling meadows, unrolled and stretched like silk-satin carpets, proliferated by multicolour flowers like the edelweiss. As for the other colourful alpine flowers that we used to gather with my children, during our picnic tours, such as the Erinus with their pink and violet colour, the Violet Cress (Ionopsidium) so white on the green grass, not to forget the multicoloured Saxifraga, mostly flowering on spring time; while at the end of autumn and early spring, we have the String of Pearls (Lobelia erinus) of white pink, red light and dark blue colours. Most of these flowers, besides fascinating my sight and decorating my home-interior, were also main ingredients in my health products, for their fragrance and important natural nutrients.

I sat on the edge of the cliff overlooking the lake with its splendid mystical sight, whence I was detached from my group who were still talking overwhelmed in their conspicuous and attractive plans. Of course, the incentive motivator, the impetus, was my husband, always innovative and ambitious seeking new endeavours, and achievements, any issue he comes up with or sees!

I was getting more and more loosened up, the heaviness on my legs were almost gone, the cool clean air was already playing its magic on my body, especially my lungs which were mitigated trying to get rid of the toxin – nicotine – even though I did not smoke cigarette, yet my passivity did not change much of the situation regarding my lungs. Taking advantage of our (Mrs. Jun Hua and I) polite and lenient attitude, the cigarette addicts including my husband had a free hand and inconsiderate position that we had to bear all along our trip.

Chinese men in general were heavy smokers and that propagation amazed me. It was so common, work-a-day routine, almost all adults, especially older people, smoked and puffed cigarettes of native products. No need to say that foreign blends were appreciated. I noticed that even in the most rural far-stretched regions, people did smoke cigarettes. I even saw, in some central and north towns of China, people using water-pipes with pure tobacco, like the ones I had seen in Middle Eastern countries. I remember with great nostalgia the souvenir of my parents having used water-pipe, smoking it from time to time. I presume it was the Mongol influence, who introduced this kind of tobacco smoking centuries back, as well as many other commodities and customs, especially in culinary art.

The sky so empowered and high was already engulfed in its waters. I could see its reflections from the uncovered surface of the water; as for the other sections of the sky, they were intermingled in the huge leaves of water lilies and the nearby bamboo branches and reeds of innumerable count, stretched and cramped, in spots where even the sun lights were refracted impervious and rigid. We were making now a trinity: the earth, the cosmos, and me. Whence, the reflection of my tangible being was in the water. I was almost touching the ebb of the water. I was being impelled to it, as if there was a voice calling me. At that moment, I was seeing all those bamboo and reeds which were encircling the deep ends of the lake, thus drawing a natural line making a vegetative bay that was to engulf and protect the water lilies from the slightest tides and intruders around the vegetation. Watching all these reeds compelling and inordinately spread, I remembered a thought of Pascal, a French philosopher and mathematician who has said that "Mankind is like a reed, the most feeble of nature, but a thinking reed." Well, I am sure he had his reasons to jump to such conclusions, while I thought at that moment looking at the lotuses' mystic and prodigal blossom. We should resemble a lotus, open, spacious and serene, so ephemeral yet so alive, in one word, all in one and same species to encounter the unknown, the inexplicable about beauty, death, and rebirth.

The group at last could spot me, joyful and enchanted they came to join me realising that I was trying to enter the lake and did not know how to proceed. Seeing the sides of the water so muddy, I could not find a path, which will elongate till the reeds and the lotuses. My husband pronounced the same words of fear and caution, but I had already made up my mind on the issue summoned up my desire to get hold of that big purple lotus, and to carry with like a token of cosmic blessing a reverberation that I wanted absolutely to experience. Well, now my desire was rendered public, and of course, who of those gentlemen would refuse or not try to fulfil the desire of a woman who was in love among others, with their flower! Suddenly I had many helping hands and several ways drawn to find a path, to pave a safe coasting to get me closer to the dwelling of the lotus. My husband was insisting that I come out of the lake to leave our friends deal with the question. But on the other hand, I was insisting on the fact that my ardent pleasure was to get it myself. Our friend Mr. Chen, tall and agile with a flexible corpulence, threw himself in the move to carry out and contrive my desire. He started to advance in the water putting his legs on high stones that were coming up from the surface of the water, and stretching his hand. He asked me to follow him on his steps. I did as instructed, and acknowledged him as my leader, because he knew very well what he was doing. Whence for the first time I was touching a hand which was there for me sincere and proud. So we advanced quietly and duly. We were now very close to the lotuses, their leaves were caressing my bare feet and giving me a strange sensation of cold caress, arousing in my head a kind of mystical and dazzling feelings that made my heart beat to accelerate. Now the water was reaching almost my knees, and the lotus that I was intending to pick was still quite far-reaching. The problem was the same for my friend too. We had to make a quick decision if we wanted to soak our entire body in the lake. We had a quick eye-touch to tell each other that the lake is deep now, if that lotus was to be cut from its cradle, to be pampered in the hands of an alien woman. Initially for me it was a desire already fixed in my soul, ready to be executed ever since I met the sight. But for Mr. Chen, the problem was to be studied from another angle. His manly ego and his prestige were at stake, therefore not one stepped back, he had to bring to success on an unconditional fact. As for me, I was starting to doubt my desire finding out that I had pushed too much, but on the other hand, I wanted to touch that flower with my own hands and overhaul its exterior beauty as well as its biological component because my scientific mind was always there, walking hand in hand with my subjective feelings. Mr. Chen got in the water, which now was reaching almost his chin, he was almost swimming, giving strong brass hands. Encouraged by my leader, I was in the water, with a sound, whose echo feared all the feeble creatures and birds perched on the trees untouchable and free. To cut short on my husband's reclamation, I feigned giving the impression having lost my balance, I fell in the lake. In reality I was drawn by a premeditated strong impulse, the water and the lotus who could resist! Indeed it was an attitude of collaboration and co-operation. Inside I was laughing, since I loved water and its contact ravished my spirit and cooled my body and ravished my thirsty heart, giving me an unprecedented joy whose memory I cherish every time I have to encounter a similar situation. I could hear my friends' and my husband's astonishment with words of desolation for having sank and plummeted in the water. They were shouting and pronouncing words of attention and precaution, meanwhile they were walking parallel to our direction in a position to run to rescue in case there was a need. Mr. Chen and I were diving and swimming with our clothes on, a sensation that I had never had before. Now I was starting to pull and push the big spherical leaves of the lotuses to pave the way to reach to my purple blossom. At last we reached the exact spot. The next big problem was how to cut that flower and its leaf since their stems were thick and soft which did not facilitate our job to detach the flower from her umbilical cord. Well my friend could take care of that too. Unfortunately we had to go back no matter how much I was trying to linger on. I started laughing inside foreseeing their embarrassment finding out our wet clothes, sticking to our bodies, thus creating a blush-making awkward situation which was not at all in their imagination neither in the programme. I was applauded because I predicated my motive for sharing my curiosity towards the unknown exotic beauty.

When we came out of the water, each carrying a lotus, we had an entrancing mood. My husband was trying desperately to find something to wipe my face. The colleagues of Mr. Chen went back to the car to fetch a towel to dry our outfits. I sat on the floor, the weather was taking care of my cloths. I started watching the flower which was now "my flower" with the acquisition and blessing of my friend Mr. Chen. Overhauling my flower attentively I could notice so many rows of petals stalk out, in a very precise and orderly way, thus each row of petals getting taller, hiding very closely the calyx, so interesting with its corolla of golden yellow pollens at the centre. Now another problem was bothering me — how to bring this flower to Nanjing in a healthy state to make it live for some days, if not for a week till I go back to Zurich. The flower on the floor lying on its big leaf was smiling at me under the last rays of the sun. I felt happy that I had been initiated for the second time, owing to the fact that I reached to a certain self-realisation through my constant visits to China and I had been ordained in its clear water, in a no man's land, among the most chimerical fabulous flowers and reeds whose unexposed "intelligence" drew and encompassed me to be initiated among their happy enclave of enchanting waters.

Shanghai

"Xintiandi"

This was the spirit of Shanghai in the 1980s, *xintiandi* meaning "new earth and sky." The former President Jiang Zemin, before becoming president of all China, was the mayor of Shanghai where he had made a statement on his view on material richness, by adding that – to become rich is to be glorious. Based on this concept he pushed his hometown to transform into a powerful financial city, thus he created an entirely new city within Shanghai, the "Pudong."

Shanghai thus became or re-established the economic capital of China. The modern city with its new buildings, high skyscrapers, shopping centres, modern museums and post-modern opera house and not to forget the underground system – the world's most commercial magnetic levitation train, designed by the French – that will be linked to the airport. Unfortunately they are tearing down hundreds of old buildings too, to replace with more and more new and attractive premises. In one word, the patrimony is somehow losing its value, considering to the fact that it is not bringing money. In any case Shanghai always considered itself as the financial and cultural capital of China. The people of Shanghai were always sophisticated, very international, and always willing for novelty and the new did inspire them.

But the Shanghai I visited some 26 years ago was so different from the new Shanghai of the 21st century with its shocking pace.

I remember the first time I visited Shanghai. I did not see much of the city since the main roads that we had to cross to reach our hotel were quite large. I must admit they all looked the same to me, nothing attractive, rather shabby and dark pavements, crossing from time to time crinkly side streets without any vegetation. People on side roads were busy coming and going, mostly on their bicycle, too many of them, nothing colourful of the typical "Chinese" the way I was imagining, colourful full of brouhaha with many shops around. There were no special lights illuminating the city. Already when we were landing, it must have been ten o'clock in the evening. I was surprised to see that the city was in the dark, as if everybody was sleeping and they had to put down their light. But then how about the street lights or the colourful bulbs of advertisement of the lights that decorate the movie theatres, I could not observe anything of the sort. Everything was grey and the hot cloudy damp atmosphere was not helping to improve the morose and dull scenery that was running before my eyes. Honestly Guangzhou seemed much more happy and colourful than Shanghai, during my visits to both cities at the same period of time. In Guangzhou there were many more boutique style shops on the corner of small streets, compared to the friendly stores in Shanghai, where for many years I had to be content and accept to do my shopping. There were no coffee shops, no kiosks on the main streets. There were high walls of cement of some 4-5 meters which remind me of the historic city walls on a modern version.

Peace Hotel in those days was the best in town, where all foreigners would take down. The hotel had no stars, as it is customary for all hotels in the world to designate the quality and the standard of the hotel. There was no other hotel to compete or to be discerned with and try to be excelled of. Competition was not there, they could enjoy by and large to disregard our comfort. Already we could observe the slow but firm improvements with this hotel, where at each time we were putting up there would be some renovation taking place, either changing the carpets, or the curtains, adding bathrooms and so on. But consecutively and duly all the advancement to the better were there, especially the concept of cleanliness and hygiene were taking a good consideration and infiltrated in the morals, manners and habit of the staff. The hotel was situated on Nanking Road, the most historically renowned road that met the muddy Huangpu River, which is the sister river or a tributary of the Yangtze. The colour was so reddish brown that would leave me perplexed each time I would cross it, leaving me in a mood which would inhibit and retain my illusion and desire from swimming in it, notwithstanding the presence of rusty boats and cargo ships of the city as a very important port.

historic Shanghai

All cities have a history and that history is told with much eloquence if the city's contemporary history is of high importance. Well this is the case with the city of Shanghai which was built around the Huangpu River. It was first a fishing village in the 10th century. Its name indicated "on the sea," its ideal geographic natural situation prepared its way to what we know today as the new Shanghai, a crossroad for its economical and tourist invasion. More than one million tourists flock towards Nanking Road every day. The Nanking Road, originally built for horsemen, was called the "Great *Malu*" or the "Great horse road." By the middle of the 16th century, the people of Shanghai built a high wall and a moat to protect themselves from the invasion of pirates. I had seen some remnant of those walls still erect till the 1980s. At the beginning of the 19th century, we can see the influence of the foreigners, especially the Europeans: first the British, then French, Japanese, Americans, and white Russians, who had established colonial concessions. I have seen those European-style buildings empowering over the eastern end of Nanking Road.

In 1842 in a treaty called "the Treaty of Nanking" by which most of that section, the area of Nanking Road, was ceded to foreigners and left under their domination, polemic and ill till today. We can see the European influence in the French town where I could see Victorian-style brick villas and Tudor style semi-detached villas, also high 12-storey mansion blocks, some of these mansions were ravaged during the Cultural Revolution. And the unfortunate thing is that so many of such buildings are being planned to be demolished to build up building to re-house millions of residents in the modern blocks.

At the beginning of the 20th century round the years of 1920-30s Shanghai was renowned for being a city of pleasure and fun. It had become the centre of vice, drugs, and prostitution, in one word, visited by gangsters and intellectuals; a modern metropolis attracting all kinds of people – sailors, gamblers, swindlers, the new rich and the very poor. People from everywhere would come to Shanghai to enjoy night life, including Europeans as well as people from other Asian countries. From the 1950s to 1970s Shanghai was lagged, not keeping the pace, but in a decade it changed again, to overshadow and tower the old colonial waterfronts across the Huangpu River.

Shanghai today with its incessant rising provides the charm of the old and the new city. This is what makes the allurement and appeal of Shanghai, notwithstanding the same reality works with other Chinese metropolis. The city of Pudong mostly grew around the east of the Huangpu River and Puxi remains the old city which was built on the west side of the Huangpu River. Through the years changes were multiplying. The government brought a big change to the city, whose repercussions and huge evidence are so amazingly and proudly demonstrated. Shanghai can boast of its nickname as Paris of the Far East, not only for its extravagant buildings and contemporary architecture, but also for its coffee shops, new five-star hotels, casinos, shopping centres, department stores, horse racing, public gardens, and museums. Shanghai people are fun loving and curious in nature, compared with other cities in China. More adapting to the times and cultivating their fun loving attitude and feeling, fashion conscious and modern in their attire, notwithstanding trying to modernise their physical appearance too, following the latest technology for better days or to enhance to that end by working harder and being ambitious.

They are smart under the leadership of a very powerful and brilliant man who knew the value of money and emphasised to its fellow citizens that earning money was a worthwhile challenge. After such statements it is hard not to move towards that goal and to measure their pulse and heart beat through money. They were going to acquire higher studies and be able to go abroad, henceforth with money they were to correct their faces in case they wanted to resemble to the Occidental man and woman. So money was the essence of all endeavours. It was the bread, the water, and the salt, it was the force which was to ignite their sunshine and make the moon yellow. It was no more a taboo subject; or the contrary was the conspicuous reality. The more they talked, the more it was in the minds and hearts.

Our days in Shanghai were planned always through the pearl corporation. They would come with two cars engineered in China. We would go to their premises which was situated in the old city quite far. But to my regret they were planning to move to the west side of Nanking Road, which was going to facilitate in many ways their daily programme.

Of course, personally I had no complaints of this daily transport. It was not a bother the way our friends were deducing, considering the fact it was giving me the opportunity to cross the inner city thus having more insight of Shanghai life or rather the street life.

Initially the rooms in the premise had very high ceilings. They were buildings left by foreigners. If we cleaned away the disorder, the rooms would spread their normal space in all grace, not undermining the fact that they were nicely decorated with curved motifs all around the walls and in the middle of the ceiling with 19th century European taste and art. Since our corporation was dealing with many commodities from many different provinces, the offices were full of all kinds of precious and semi-precious stones, jewellery, furnitures, Christmas decorations, art flowers, and mostly their very famous porcelain vases and dinning sets, carpets from Teitsin, to name a few; an abundance which could not leave me indifferent. There were so much exuberance of art and craft in one building, which had to be exported to different destinations. Having been to Russia many times, I could not see or even compare the richness of that one building to the whole market of Moscow's main commercial streets or department store. This is China a surprisingly different continent not to be compared or measured!

Initially we were in the 1980s. Yet China needed to compete with the other Asian countries. Of course she was not that new on the market, but she was new to play the free market. She had yet to establish a profile and to acquire a decent place in the world market. Their marketing force was weak or almost did not exist. There existed no contract or rather very irrelevant compared to the international standard. They believed more on oral agreements and mutual respect than on signed paper that could be changed and disrespected regarding the momentum and the place. Chinese had to learn to organise their factories and to quote correct prices for each continent. Things were moving fast. We were personally paying the price of these incessant changes that were shaping the face of the new ascending China.

The outside world was pressuring China to walk towards openness, to have a free hand to the world economy. China was eager to join the world economy. Times were auspicious to comply to the world market. China had to implement and endorse new ratification; new rules and structures were imposed on the people; so the social face of the urban and rural people were gradually changing. This kind of situations brought forth new social status quo, a new condition and state of affairs based on moderation and openness for foreign businessmen as well as for the natives. The social influence of China was eminent because of their historic influence and their colossal number in population, which could not be undermined; therefore social changes were eminent assessment. America and Europe tried at the beginning of the twentieth century to undermine this reality, but it was the position of the ostrich head in the sand! China was a polar star whose gleam was reaching the earth. Countries had to change binoculars to establish their position in the cosmic family to reside with the other stars and to let their gleam be absorbed by the other binoculars. How much more could they deny the reality of its potential?!

Our corporation was nervous, because many factories outside Shanghai were willing to make direct contract with their clients. This is how our itinerary shifted towards other cities and other provinces, meanwhile keeping in touch and through the guidance of our corporation, from one day to the other had to play the middle-men in their own country, arranging and organising the sales between the Chinese corporations, the factories, and ourselves. This kind of rather unprecedented situation brought forth a circle of newly rich people, who took advantage of the situation, and created rivalry and competition within the different corporations. Enterprising and encouraging the law of the jungle or should I say the order of the zoo!

It was the state of the modern era, the free pecuniary monetary state. I understand and respect the calculated steps of the Chinese government in adjusting the Chinese economical system, relying on the competence of its many material premiere, natural richness, and manpower, creative power and intelligence. I do not see how and on what basis you can impair or have a prejudice and be conceited of a country who has got such a potential, an inherent latent aptitude as big as the world. The only thing that China did not have was the modern advanced technique. I admit a very important issue, a very important point in the huge modernisation plan of Shanghai and Beijing. As if you had the body of the car made of silver but you did not know how to install the wheels, since the technical issue to mount the wheel of the car could not yet reach or comply to the required international standard. So China depended on the Occidental technique, and nobody can deny this fact. But the mirror has to face the counterparts of the proficient products which are manufactured in China, with the consideration and the agreement of the exported countries. My husband and I were somehow squeezed in this kind of quick shifting policy; our endeavours impaired, our attempts and all our efforts seemed like a drop of water in this ocean of newcomers. They were big vessels, attractive, full of lure and enticement, having the potential to sail even with bigger strides, to reach the port of their hanker.

At each trip I had to encounter a new phase in Shanghai. The streets were getting more dense, people on each pavement, an unprecedented human tide, thus making one to realise how populated our world has become. People were wearing more colourful clothing of diversified design. Gradually bicycles were giving way to more cars, mostly native product made in China; and around the 1990s I met quite a few Mercedes Benz, some Range Rovers, and Japanese and American cars. And something that enchanted me was the presence of those trottoir-cafés that years back I could have never imagined. Shanghai is a belt between the modern and new China, the China which was running and the China which was slowing down the clock to have and respect its leisurely moments. Because Shanghai people have "la joie de vivre" – something that I apprehended later on. Once again I conceived and actualised that a country has a trait of character, which shapes his every-day life. The people of Shanghai are one of those group or countrymen that like to indulge and feel happy and free to organising their everyday lives, a concept that I conceived during my frequent visits. I can substantiate my predilection by bringing in and telling you my story that happened in Shanghai.

It must have been the beginning of the 1980s. We were again with our children visiting Shanghai paying a call on all the major cities of the Pearl Road. My children were most of the time with us touring the city. Unfortunately sometimes they were repeatedly calling in at the premises of the corporation which had to enhance my children another perception and another impression, a view-point regarding the trip and its different contribution based on "human relation," since being always with some of the members of the corporation made them closer to the Chinese character, and accordingly get closer to the general feeling.

One evening, I was sitting with the children at the lobby of the hotel waiting for my husband to join us. We were attracted by the sound of music from a nearby room. It was not Chinese music, of course even that would have surprised us, but it was western music, a melody of the 1960s, notes playing something like a Tango. No need to say we were like bees attracted to the pollen of flowers in a big garden. This melody was so alluring and comely to our ears that all of us stood up. And as if a magnet was pulling us, we started to follow the waves of the music. The more we were walking, the stronger the music was getting. At last we came in front of a door where the music was stronger as we knocked to be polite, but we did not get any reaction, obviously the pounding of the music was so strong that there was no way someone could have heard us from inside. Therefore I turned the knob of the door and to my big surprise I saw a small orchestra at one corner of a rather big room playing music. When they saw us standing there, flabbergasted, right away they stopped, and with an amusing face invited us to come in. That's what we did. Next we tried to find some chairs at the back of the room, to make ourselves comfortable. They restarted playing one music after another, and we were so overwhelmed and emotions got so high that suddenly I threw myself along with my children at the centre of the room which was to become our dancing floor. On this our musicians, all native Shanghai people, were so happy that they started to give more tempo to their concert by playing more modern and contemporary music.

The next day we woke up a little tired, but all radiating with happiness. It was one of my most memorable days that I had in China considering my long trips for more than two decades. When we went down for breakfast, we saw some of the dancer visitors like us, whom we had not noticed beforehand. They were all friendly, and the indifference among us was extinguished. We were no more timid and shy, the iceberg had melted through the heat of the night; ready to exchange visit cards or try to remember our first names. Unfortunately we did not meet our musicians on that trip; we were told later on that they were a group of amateur players and they were practising some of their music. On my next trip to that same hotel, this time alone with my husband, that same group was there! They were giving concerts of light music on the weekends. Similar to any other dancing club in the West, we were served drinks and even cold dine.

Shanghai gave us many souvenirs and successful business endeavours.

My children had to take with them along many alluring moments a very unique and irreplaceable present. It was in one of their visits that the corporation send a very prominent young sculptor to carve the busts of my three children. This was a token and a big present that the corporation could assess to express their deep appreciation towards these three teenagers for being friendly, cordial, and appreciating by being receptive to their environment, behaving well, and enjoying the new with deference and ardour. No need to say the extend of our pride, my husband and I, we were deeply touched by this solicitude. I do not know if in those days my children really grasped the value of that present, but today after so many years, they care about those carved statues so much that each had to carry with to their homes.

Pearl Forum

We had been cordially invited by our Beijing head office to go to Dalian to attend a forum about the pearl and its marketing situation. Dalian is a city in the northeast of China facing the Pacific Ocean. This was our first visit to Dalian for all of us, including my husband.

The day we first landed at the airport the weather had a warm maritime mood dispersing a continental monsoon climate, very typical of that region. The gentle fresh air blowing in the air was like a caress to our faces, awakening my senses and my conscious mind to the smell of the maritime heavy humid air, mixed up with sand and salt. My children were happy and thrilled. Dalian, I was told, is a city with a history of only one hundred years old. Since its foundation, it is in full expansion culturally and economically in an incredibly high speed. It has many industries such as chemical, metallurgy, petroleum refinery, textile, food, and electronics; also agricultural products; and today it holds a festival for clothing. This explains the presence of so many Japanese in the city and their influence in the modernisation and its economical output. It had a mountainous landscape with plenty of green space. I heard there were some temples up there on the mountain of Shengshui, as for the other mountains such as Paotai Shan, Xijian Mountain, and Tahai Mountain so mysterious and impressive. It is my ardent desire to climb one day one of those mountains. For the time being, I am still hiking the Swiss mountains, hoping to find the auspicious time to make my dream come true. Today Dalian has got another face. It is deployed and set up a seaport city, a port with an outstanding capacity, as far as ranking the third port in China by its importance.

We had boarded from Beijing to reach Dalian. My husband had told me that there was a forum to be held; a very big gathering of pearl dealers from all over the world, especially from Japan. A forum on behalf of the pearls to debate and discuss its situation in the world market and the ways to control quality and quantity. Having in mind that for some time many other countries around the world were producing and culturing pearls, there was an urgent need not to dump more prices, to halt the output and to enhance a better quality to the output. Of course this was a very important gathering which was going to have a big impact on the pearl business later on. At last I was telling my husband that dealers and producers should come together to act mutually to protect what is known as the queen. Many bankruptcies were taking place due to these inordinate uncontrollable production, bringing down prices and filling the market more than it could absorb. I was happy and very proud that finally all our endeavours were being considered seriously. Farmers, corporations, big producers, pearl dealers and merchants were coming together to debate and mutually compromise to implement a just marketing tag, to enhance a better transaction for the future of this sensitive business.

At the Golden Beach

Dalian is a golden beach and I am sure today it can match the best European Riviera, given its clean waters and its sandy beaches, not polluted with its technological rush.

I spend whole afternoons swimming in that sea and relaxing on the sand under the two attentive and timid members of the corporation, as our bodyguards.

They stood there in their long trousers and white shirts under the blazing sun confronting the heat and the fun, accompanied the cheer and delight of my children. They were not persons of beguile, in their way they were sharing the merriment of their new friends who were yelling and screaming out of pleasure at the touch of the low tide's cold and crystal clear waters, washing up their warm feet covered with the muddy sand, the cheerful echo of those teenage friends coming from the other continent.

At night there was a welcoming banquet at the honour of the foreign guests. No need to say about the gorgeous and lavish dressed tables of the Chinese banquets; from north to south, east to west, every city I visited from the smallest to the biggest, they all had the same approach, the same generosity. This is China, an unequalled hospitality and generosity of good taste and creativity in every subject and on every issue. Exquisite tasty food, lavish, full of variety, not being capable to enumerate all the various gourmet dishes that we had to taste and the different drinks in our cups. Those were remembrances of unequalled enticement, an inveigle that even kings would become envious of.

Unfortunately the outcome of the symposium was not very prominent, since it took many more meetings and discussions to shape up, adjust and exonerate the major constraint and exigency of the different parties.

We left a few days later. We flew over the sea, and I looked down at Dalian from my window and realised how small it looked from high up in the sky, compared to the big role it had pertained down on earth-bound problems.

Beijing, the Elegant Strait-laced Capital

Beijing is the capital of China par excellence, and it's said capital certifies its major status as the most important and eminent city of the country. Invoking feeling and the very distinct comportment of its citizens, who have the pride and gratification to belong and be associated to the capital.

Beijing denotes the pulse and the strength of its nation, all echoes of such demeanours, airs and manners have to hurl from its ground; to carry most of the aspect of the economic welfare; and they are the ones who have to do most of the concessions, henceforth to carry the weal and the woe. And proud citizens, who are conscious of these realities, succeeded beyond any doubt to become the prominent subtle rulers of the whole country. This stance is true for all capitals and hence bears the name as the most rewarding city and its citizens as the gratified forbearing persons. No need to say that at each of my trips the city was changing its inner structures. I say inner structure because the centre was unchanging due to the presence of the very famous and wonderful antique palaces of Beijing, the "Forbidden City" at the heart of the city facing Tian'anmen Square, one of the most famous squares in the world like the famous "Red Square" in Moscow. Tian'anmen Square became famous ensuing the day Chairman Mao inaugurated the birth of the People's Republic of China in 1949. We can see his portrait hanging there at the gate, very alive and imposing picture, spreading shade of respect. A little bit further is the Great Hall of the People. All these had a singular allure and different atmosphere, a mood of richness and power that you cannot feel or seize in any other city in China; there is a flow of energy that I could feel rarely in any other spots in the country. A distinguished city keeping the same profile in its new pace of modernisation, Beijing from the time I visited it some decades ago, had outlined a physical change out of recognition; with the new flashy modern buildings, corporate restaurants and hotels. It has become a city of steel and stone and plexi-glass. Unfortunately historic buildings were being razed to give way to these new developments.

My husband and I inaugurated the opening of the "Sheraton", a five-star hotel. At each trip we could sight two to three other world-famous chain hotels; and each time there was more fluke of tourists to fill these beautiful hotels, popped up like mushrooms at every corner of the city. This kind of booming reminded me of Japan in the beginning of the 1970s, the time of its openness towards the outside world.

There are two types of visitors in China in general, from America and Australia as corporate merchants or technicians. As for the native tourists in their own country, their main presence is that they are visiting Beijing for its attractive economical status, buying power on all kinds of commodities, competitive quality and price. On the other hand, being attracted and curious about its history, powerful and empirical, its antique sights, most of them renown monuments, palaces, temples, reciting the history of a big nation, impregnated with instructive tradition pervaded with beauty and culture, wisdom and intelligence, power and dominance, conspicuous and compelling, commanding and prevailing authority, claiming to be the oldest empire in world history. Many powerful empires like Egypt, Persia, Rome, Macedonia, Mameluke of the Arabs, and Ottoman Turkey played eminent roles and extinguished, but the Chinese Empire and later on the republic as a holistic power and sovereign state sustained the changes, the invasion of the Occidentals, and the civil wars.

Looking Ahead by Looking Back

On this issue of modernising and getting rich, the Chinese compare today's modernisation programme to the Tang Dynasty's golden age. The Tang Dynasty was a very prosperous period. During its time, many things prospered, such as Taoism and Buddhism. There was also the blossoming in various fields such as poetry, medicine, astrology, and architecture. Chinese history books blame its downfall to its rapid growth in Buddhism and also foreign influences. Following the example, she must protect herself from chaos and upheaval, to maintain a durable, strong, balanced, and modern country.

Every time I revisit Beijing, I am faced with a new changing face of the city, the absence of familiar landmarks with the disappearing *hutong*s where you could find aligned teahouses, street markets, noodle shops, little shops where street vendors used to sell leaf-wrapped dumplings from steamers, old ladies selling fruits in their baskets. All the disappearance were due to rapid changes and I am concerned with these rapid changes, where whole communities are transient and drifting, their centres disappearing, having been demolished to rebuild new modern buildings. Of course, on the other hand, many people are impressed and happy about the quick modernisation of the capital, thus influencing the other cities.

The future of Beijing is bright. There is no hesitation about that conspicuous reality. People are more concerned with moneymaking and enhancing an alluring and attractive immediate programme of living with more promising modernised programme, rather than preserving the local architectural heritage like *hutong*s. To understand better the basis of the Beijing demographic design and strategy of the architecture, I have to go back to history.

Beijing is designed with alleys or *hutong*s (lanes). There are several thousand of *hutong*s in Beijing. Many were built during the 13th century with the Yuan Dynasty. *Hutong*s grew larger with the Ming Dynasty, continuing with the Qing Dynasty.

The *hutongs*

All the *hutong*s near the royal palace were neat and orderly and most of the residents of these *hutong*s were residing imperial kinsmen and aristocrats. Ensuing further more to the north and south from the centre were the simple *hutong*s with their modest dwellings, mostly made for merchants and simple folks.

I could see the *hutong*s' main buildings with roof beams and pillars all beautifully curved and painted with front yard and back yard. Almost all quadrangles were composed of four houses around a courtyard. Very typical big quadrangles were designed and occupied by high-ranking officers or rich merchants. Whence the lesser the status of the occupant, the smaller the quadrangle would be and further and narrower the *hutong*.

The most amazing story for me is the progression and expansion of these *hutong*s which would tell the history and evolution of their times. The social changes of modern China were also reflected on their dwellings. Therefore the neat and organised pattern of the *hutong*s was affected. There were no more regular houses, the quad-rangles once occupied by one family were occupied by many households. Fortunately we can still find many *hutong*s in Beijing, which have survived the changes, giving Beijing the charm of the modern, yet ancient city.

The residential area of Beijing has its lanes and alleys of hundreds of years old. They are not altogether metamorphosed and razed, even though the city is developing into a modern international metropolis. They are still serving and housing half the urban population not to forget the old fashion pedicab and markets and small private shops.

This is why Beijing's construction program for the 2008 Olympic Games is highly supervised by the government under strict regulations already proffered to preserve historic and cultural sites, relics, and the dwellings around the *hutong*s' historical sites.

An article said that the city has been spending a colossal amount of money in the past three years in projects for protecting and renovating many more hundreds of historical and cultural sites such as the upcoming renovation of the Forbidden City alone is going to cost the government about 84 million dollars.

Coming to Meet Authentic Natives of *hutong*

One day I stayed at the hotel and let my husband go with the corporation. I thought it was the best occasion to execute my plan to make an excursion in the old *hutong*s to come across real people, authentic Chinese people in their everyday life. I summoned all my courage and decided to be out alone, China and I, without my husband or a friend to guide me, for the sake of translation or protection.

I knew the centre and around well, but the point at issue was to reach around there, since at each visit to Beijing, we came to different hotel, or walking always to the city from different ways, taking short cuts or highways; notwithstanding the fact that I was sitting at the back of cars and not driving myself, would not let me bridge the avenues and the streets to the sight, spots and the visited areas.

The day was sparkling, a breeze was blowing, bringing forth fresh air from the nearby forest, ensuing a bright warm atmosphere, a cloudless sky. It was an auspicious day, no burning sun. I put on my baskets and started my marathon walk. I felt so good, so light-spirited that my heart was leaping out and if I was given a new propulsion, I was sure I could fly given the momentum. I had such an impetus and energy that I categorically excluded the possibility to take a taxi. I wanted to walk and find my way. According to the hotel's desk, I must not be very far from the centre. And she advised me to look for the taxis waiting for tourists. I thanked her for her help, and drew out of the hotel's door. Actually my ardent expectation was to find some freedom to be led through my own itinerary and my own predilection towards an issue each time I visited Beijing or other arias in China to know how and who resides in the far end *hutong*s, an enticement to experience personally their true atmosphere, an environment without any influence, an informative background of true people in their everyday life. I must have walked two hours when I started to get closer to traffic and the sight of irregular alleys. I left the wide road and followed a turning edge which brought me suddenly parallel with a very narrow alley. I stood there for a while and looked around and got in as if I was being propelled by the time machine in the realms of history. The more I was walking, the more the image was getting strange. I was on a rather populated street. I was telling myself persons of recent history, seeing many little kids playing around under the heat, encouraging me to advance more, no feeling of strangeness, only a feeling of curiosity was to brim over my heart, and ample deep down to pervade my innermost desire to meet convivial people and engage a conversation, but how and with whom? Adults were also scrutinising me and nodding their heads, a simple gesture of welcome. I continued my way; I was running to fulfil and assign my aspiration, an avid yearning all one wants. Again I stopped, this time I was hearing the cry of hen and the soft voice of a woman singing. I tried to get closer to the entrance from where I heard the note reaching to my ear. I stood in front of high walls that had parapets and battlements on the top. It looked more like a ruin than a palace, but one could guess that it was the remnants of an old mansion so much heard about. Actually I had seen similar mansions, impressively big like château, well-kept compounds around the rich areas of the city. This time I continued walking a little bit more, till I reached a big porch, leaning to high columns of stone covered with greyish white earth. I stretched my head looking inside with great curiosity, and I saw a very big courtyard enclosing a compound building of quadrangular architecture with and around courtyard houses or what remains of a house. I got in, without hesitation. Suddenly I was not timid or baffled. I was in the middle of a courtyard with no decoration or vegetation. In one look one could say it was indeed in bad shape, untidy and inept, with many agricultural utensils dispersed here and there. The song had stopped, so did I. Suddenly I took notice of my courageous act, realising that I was in a private property and no more in the street. Someone talked to me in Chinese, but of course I could not understand, therefore I talked with the language of Shakespeare and this time as an answer I saw a rather young woman accompanied of an old man, who were walking towards my end. On a quick reflex knowing that I was maybe vexing the owners or even annoying them, I walked one step backward and waited. Their rather kind tone stopped me and instead I made an effort to walk towards their end. Now I was so close to them that I could well observe their features and distinguish their different attire from the usual Chinese I meet during my visits.

The old man smiled at me, the most beautiful smile ever, coming from a foreigner. I received the same treat from his daughter, who later on I was told was the daughter-in-law married to Mr. Sun's son, who was working in a factory of machinery, on the outskirts of the capital. The old man pointed to me a low table and invited me to sit down and asked something from her daughter. She ran towards the house keeping her joyful face like an inspiration. I sat without any hesitation. I was getting a little tired too. The old man started to talk, being conscious of the fact that I was not getting him, but he was doing that to fill in the silence through my embarrassment and to commensurate and offset his confusion and my amazement. Looking around, I surmised there were many more curious heads watching us, even the hen had stopped singing flabbergasted. I supposed some young lads were running here and there in there colourful outfits; seeing me the woman in yellow hair so unusual for them, they run pronouncing some incomprehensible words towards the other courtyard. According to the architectural basic design, there were a few of them. Seeing my spontaneous reaction, and the wild reaction of the children, he asked – through guessing, of course – if I would like to come in, pointing to their humble house, alluding to the cracks on the wall and the discarded bits and pieces odds and ends on and around the house. Docile and soliciting to his friendly invitation, I stepped towards the door of the house. If my assumptions and guessing were right, he wanted to protect me from the other curious sights, yearning to have the privilege to share this moment with a blond woman befallen from the sky! I was the intruder and I wanted to apologise for my daring curiosity and intuitive action – the only simple way to meet and get closer to the natives in true feelings in their proper environment without any coverage or mannerism.

I entered the door of that modest house made of a very special material – a mixture of cement and rice, some of the surfaces covered with dark-coloured wood, nothing to remind me of the palaces' coloured roofs or painted indoors with yellow red or lapis blue. The impressive high ceilings and the extensive large living room took me by surprise. Encouraged by my guests, I walked in bigger pace to get to the living room, thus get closer and alight more their household.

Once inside, the paradox was emerging from those walls and floors. Neat floors covered with small mats and carpets of pastel colour. A very big sofa made with wood curved lace like designs was the main centre piece in that half dim room, followed by big armchairs and many closets in black lacer wood. Small tables here and there carrying some relics and Chinese books decorating most of the centre piece facing the armchairs. No need to say that with one glance one could deduce and relinquish the past glory of that place worn through the years and not been renovated. It was almost noon and their son came. I was still drinking my cha. He introduced himself and it is the custom of the Orient to show kindness and welcoming spirit to the guest. I was lucky since the son could manage with his English, so he was the hopeful herald to give a tongue to my old host. He went on explaining upon my inquisitive questions seeing the remnants of an elaborate past and his father a dignified and refined personality. He started to laugh, adding, "My father's name is Shou which means long life and he is ninety-three years old this year; he writes poetry and does some minor duties."

"This house we owned long times ago," he went on talking, "but today is inhabited with many families. My father was a big merchant, undertaking the routes of Silk Road till Beijing, a thriving family business till 1911 the Republic of China which broke his business!" I was so much into the talk that I did not see a dressed table behind in the adjacent room with fancy meal dressed on a neat tablecloth. By the way, Beijing is known for its Beijing Duck – a food very difficult to prepare.

I left that family being treated like a real guest. They made me eat the best. They had an open-handed and generous family, a representative of four generation I thanked them for their kindness and the avid illustrations, exactly having lived my expectations like a miracle. For me they were exactly the image that China was denoting – a family that experienced the vicissitude of life. The old man, the most loving character, was very much attached to his past relics, and was proud of them, while the new generation including his elder son who fought under Cultural Revolution, denied and ignored those relics. Notwithstanding the younger generation in that household was more open, and realistic about our world. Therefore exonerated the issue of those palaces and pagodas only as a history and ruins of pride while they were happy to have so mady revolutions that readjust and brought forth a modern and strong China. As for the teenagers in the house, they had jeans and made up and looked very modern in that old house. But amazingly enough, the traditional customs were always kept, including with the new generation and those girls and boys were my witness. Tradition is a national issue too, highly respected but not in the same context or contrived in the same manner. All the festivals and traditional feasts are celebrated like the lantern festival or the spring festival to name a few.

For me as a foreigner, I admired their past and appreciated their present modern creative and diligent spirit, rewarding and committed, assessed to bring forth many industries in petro-chemical branch, in biochemical branch, in high tech, in different commodities, in food industry, porcelain, last but not least their herbal medicine, silk embroideries, the carpets to name a few a colossal gigantic present which will stretch to a promising future.

Forbidden City

As for me, the adventurous voyager, I could not close my chapter on Beijing, without writing my concise impressions on some of the famous monuments of the city such as the Forbidden City (called Gu Gong in Chinese), a palace in rectangular shape located on Tian'anmen Square. It is the world's largest palace of about one kilometre long from each side. It was the imperial palace during the Ming and Qing dynasties. Commoners were not allowed to enter the city. It was built between 1406-1420 by the Ming emperors.

My husband and I had the privilege to stay overnight in one of the buildings of the palace, being the guest of the corporation. That was an experience and a treat given only to VIP people and no need to say that I did not sleep all night. First I was over excited sleeping in one of the complexes, and the other reason considering our beds were not that comfortable! A few years later, when I saw the American film *The Last Emperor*, I was so proud and thrilled telling people that we slept in one of the complexes of the palace and we have been touring a few times the palace itself.

The Forbidden City is divided into two parts with 9000 rooms. The southern section or the outer court was where the emperor exercised his supreme power. The northern section or the inner court, was where fourteen emperors of the Ming Dynasty and ten emperors of the Qing Dynasty had reigned. Having been a palace for five centuries, it became a palace museum with numerous rare treasures, marvellous painted decorations, of art and design, royal architecture of spacious magnificent halls, a reminiscence of rich powerful and prosperous past of the country. Indeed it's a huge palace, with many complexes and halls and rooms. The bricks on the walls were made from white lime and rice, while the cement was a mixture of rice and egg whites. The dominant colour in the Forbidden City is yellow, the walls are mainly red, and the roof is with gold and yellow glazed tiles, since yellow is the symbol of the royal family and amazingly enough it is also my preferred colour. So my admiration had a double sense. The decorations in the palace were either yellow or gold, including the bricks on the ground which were yellow through a special process. No one was allowed to use the colour yellow, except the emperor. Almost everything around him was yellow, including his outfit, the dishes, even his pillow cases and blankets. A magnificent place and a rich museum.

Dowager Summer Palace

I was always keen on king and queen story. When I was a littler girl, my young soul and vivid imagination was held dear on fancy fairy tales, which ended by a handsome and powerful prince, marrying a beautiful princess. Years later, I started being attracted by the beautiful majestic outfits that princesses of every country would wear; not to undermine the jewellery made of pearl, gold and precious stones. Although my predilections and preferences have changed through the years in substance and in abject pragmatic stand, yet again realistically, most of us are intrigued with the life of famous people, especially if they are people who reside in palaces. This is how my curious and earnest character towards beauty and power took me to visit the very famous palace of Dowager Empress Cixi (1835-1908). She loved power and richness. But the paradox was that during her reign China suffered economic losses! She lived in the Forbidden City, which I had visited a few times before, but she resided mostly in summer season in the "Summer Palace." She enjoyed a lavish life, having many secret lovers. Another reminiscence about her despot character, she cared for elaborate food. I was told that she ordered every day a new receipt with each meal, and many tens of them everyday, with different ingredients and taste. It is a difficult task, given the tremendous toil for the cooks, to abide to that kind of eccentric desire!

The Summer Palace comprised the most beautiful gardens and ponds decorated by the ephemeral beautiful lotuses, covering the surface of the water, like a floating garden coming out of the glass. It was surrounded with pavilions of flowers. Walking by the small tower, I was amazed to find a marble boat of actual size, which was pointing its nose to the Kunming Lake. Our guide explained that she feared water so much that she ordered to build a boat of marble, to give her the satisfaction and impression that she was boating over the lake. An amazing personality with her very long nails and jewellery, this Manchu empress was also troubled by the Westerners. Her attitude was as a reigning monarch and the destiny of the country was shaped after her. This reminds me of French King Louis the XIV at the end of the 17th century, who encouraged education and culture, erected a strong empire and also built the very famous majestic Versailles Palace. He was also a very lavish and despotic king and his grandson, Louis the XVI, paid the price of his grandfather's mistakes. During the famous French Revolution in 1789, Louis the XVI was judged by the people and decapitated with the guillotine. Pu Yi became emperor at the age of five, and was forced to abdicate the throne, becoming the last emperor of China ever.

The Great Wall

My next unforgettable experience was my visit to the Great Wall. It was a totally different monument, of another dimension and another landscape; it did not give the serenity of the Summer Palace, nor the magnificence and artful exhibition of the Forbidden City. At first look, it looked like a wall high, impressive and grey, piled up and erected, stones over stones, elongated passing and hailing five provinces and many major and important cities on its passage. They are the stone of protection of will and power; the hardship of consequential effort and endeavour of manpower, designed by architects of their times; premeditated and planned under powerful leaders. It is also the manifestation of organisation, an assessment and consecration of will; a demonstration of tenacity of the Chinese rulers and the people of China.

Its main purpose was to be built as a defensive fortification against the invaders. It was under Emperor Qin Shi Huang that the Wall was finally joined together, to defend the eminent invaders, the Huns from the North.

When I stood on the wall, the breeze was hailing me on the passage. It was an indication of power and conviction and attestation of great men of vision, generals with high projection, who could envision the mastery of the human ability.

According to astronomers, amazingly enough, the great wall is a landmark that can be viewed from the space. No doubt about it because one can feel very close to the sky once you are on the wall itself. It had a length of 6,700 kilometres from east to west like a worn out but ageless dragon of 2,000 years old who grew drawing a history of power of vicissitude, unity, and boundless energy of its people living under three different reigns of Qin, Han, and Ming dynasties drawing across its desert fields and mountains. It is undoubtedly a landmark of culture and power denoting a history of mankind of a very old uninterrupted civilisation.

Shan Hai Guan pass is where most of the fortification started under the Ming Dynasty. My husband and I could also see the Great Wall in Beijing and in Simatai 110 km northeast of Beijing. It is fabulous overlooking all the mountains and hills and the surrounding woods; such a gorgeous sight of inveigle and deco. But if you have vertigo, the way I had the first time, you must be careful, because the wall being very high and having many slopes gives you the impression of strong ascensions and descend. I even received an attestation – a sort of formality, from the tourist organisation, for having walked the wall for some hundreds of meters. I tell you it is a reward of merit and an assessment. The mystical and powerful influence of the Great Wall can be seen in the Chinese mythological tales and popular symbolism and legendary stories. One of these legends which had been spread through textbooks, folk songs and operas is the story of a lady, Meng Jiangnü, who cried bitterly over the death of her husband in the construction of the Great Wall. This alone can indicate the sentiment of the people over their assessments and commitments and their merit as one rewarding nation. Today the Great Wall is acknowledged by UNESCO in the world heritage and a patrimony to be protected by all.

Epilogue

My adventures and experiences in China were lively and spirited. Writing down some of them as a momentous breakthrough under the prerogative of China and pearl, which played the major caption and denomination leading me throughout this book.

I believe, through my different contacts, encounters and adventures, from one continent to the other. We all tend the same aspiration and desire, with different occurrence and condition, ensuing upon different ideologies and environment.

I was committed to those familiarities, and participating to their different ideologies and concept, their acceptance and predilection towards perceiving and sustaining life.

It is a prerequisite issue that some of us come to that realisation, therefore accept the givings of their lives, trying the best of themselves. Many religious leaders and philosophers praise the path of destiny, scientific predilection leans towards pragmatism, believing in the matter and objectivity rather than the concept of subjective, the non-tangible realities based on existentialistic objectiveness about the I, the individual and the prerogative issues related to that reality.

Through acquired experiences, I can jump to the conclusions about the concept of religious, philosophical and scientific issues, epitomising and exemplifying my path full of experiences of encounters, places, social and financial attributes, always hailing and tracing the new and the different. To exculpate and justify my existence, the path of my life, which was sketched, enticed and delineated to be outlined with the good and the bad, like all the four seasons of mother nature since nothing is random.

Pearl was the essence that had to ignite and illuminate my path. Through its lure and enticement, I had to enhance my endeavours however small, to a world of happiness and beauty, in other words, in the environment of jewellery. Actually on an objective stance, the world of jewellery is a happy world! Have you been to a jewellery fair or visited jewellery stores? They all have a happy enlightened mood. It needs a happy environment to come to the desire and aspiration of happy people; self sufficient persons who tend beyond their every day's monotonous toil, to be endowed with what comes from nature, harnessed through its water, earth, and air. A sad person is a person who will never tend to gratify or reward his person, indubitably never inveigle to purchase pearl or other precious jewellery.

The idea of jewellery is badly intercepted in our society, sometime denoting as ostentatious element or an excessive object that we can do without or an issue of rivalry, jeopardising relations or creating a feeling of negative impetus. Of course, all of these issues can be true with some reserve. Notwithstanding the most important is to explain and not to debate a global issue of human relation and inclination towards material, such as money and wealth and to its relation. My concern is with pearls and only pearls, their pure energy and symbol of peace to the wearer. Do you think a sad person or person with no curiosity will tend to think to buy pearls? Is it possible? Well, frankly speaking, I don't think so. Since I can extend my conclusion through my experience with dealers and customers who were indeed happy and radiant people, positive, willing to offer something out of the way, to some one they care other than themselves, enchanted souls willing to experience the human endeavour and its synergy to nature. I have always insisted on this important issue that today if we have so many variety, quantity, and quality of pearls, we owe to some wise men of vision, who enabled us, women, the possibility to wear pearls analogous to the well heeled and the privileged persons. An issue that was not conceivable some decades ago.

Before I end up my book, I have a nice reminiscence to tell you regarding this truth.

Years ago, before I met my husband, indeed I was terribly and dearly attracted to pearls, I was impelled to their unique beauty through fairy tales of kings and queens, who were ravished and spellbind to pearls the most natural gem of our nature, they were dressed in covered from head to toe. I was also impelled through big novels of pirates and merchants at the exploration and rite of pearls. At home my mother was not a good example, since she was never in possession of a pearl necklace, actually she had a few important jewels, settings in gold and diamond; even though my parents could afford to buy expensive jewels, being well off; but my father was inclined more to

buy expensive Iranian and Armenian Caucasian carpets. I had to wait some more years
to receive from college friends, my first present of imitation pearl, as an earring
mounted on 18 carat gold and a drop pearl pendent on a gold chain, it was for the
occasion of my nineteenth birthday. It was a few months before my marriage. I was
thrilled, receiving pearls through friends, who call to mind my love and inclination for
pearls; also the sensation and feeling of happiness to wear peals so close to my face was
an inspiration of beauty and femininity. I was told by my aunts that pearls would
enhance in a woman seven kind of beauty, this reality anyhow earnest in its context, it
had to cradle my soul and influence my heed towards pearls; whence I care about
beauty in everything I deal.

A few months later, I got married to John, my loving husband. I know you would say
with one stone I was hitting the man and the shells! Yes! Maybe! But at that age you
couldn't be that calculating and scheming. Of course, the matter of contention, so
pronounced and desired all through my life, was there, not to undermine the ensuing
aspect of the different manifestations, denoting factual realities, indicating the
fulfilment of those childhood desires. Ensuing the event, during my marriage
ceremony, I was wearing my maiden imitation-pearl earrings, since it had enfolded and
swathed me by coveting and embracing my long-pending dream; from the day I
received, I never parted from it, an utmost love towards my pearls, they truly meant so
much to me.

One has to realise that in those days (1960s) cultured pearls not only they were
scarce, but people in general did not have big knowledge and information about them
as of today. It needed years of apprentice and advertisement, to make people acknowl-
edge about its reality, history and different sources.

As for my imitation earring, they became a big social issue. Of course, my husband,
even though he was a pragmatic man, tried to understand the sensitive and delicate
aspect of my gesture. Not to undermine the fact that pearls in the 1960s were very
exclusive and expensive, therefore not budgeting a student. But on the other hand, he
couldn't grasp why I got married wearing them. Assuming that he had given me as an
engagement present, a whole set of pearls, not to mention my wedding gown sawn
with pearls! Finally some weeks after the wedding, he was happy and fulfilled to carry
out mounting a beautiful cultured pearl on the golden hooks of my earrings which was
holding my imitation pearls.

My reminiscence through my Chinese friends and encounters is a very dear experience. I enjoyed writing and expressing my true feelings and bearing witness about these creative and diligent people. With them the old and the new is walking hand in hand with such an artistry and subtlety that not only amazes me, also many other visitors who have been to China for so many decades.

I believe that every nation has to walk with its own character and tradition, and be proud of its heritage. Notwithstanding technology is already broadening our perspective, meanwhile circumscribe our world by ensuing the same and the similar all over, thus enhancing the idea of a certain look interfering and imposing on many areas beating about many fields, while trying to underline more and more the concept of conformity and comparability not in the act, but in the resemblance. Difference is so beautiful, it brings up curiosity, teaches us tolerance and acceptance to attend and cope with that difference, to become more receptive, broad-minded, a counterpart not always to resemble, to image, to please the other, but rather a sharing and assessing behaviour.

This is how I, the protagonist, encountered China the altruistic, and the pearl in all its expansion and splendour, in an incentive itinerary of a quarter of a century, encountered worldly-wise happy and unrivalled cherished moments, and many wonderful friends along, and always with my Johnny boy.